MacKenna's

Piece

IRVING A. GREENFIELD

MacKenna's Piece

Irving A. Greenfield

Blueberry Lane Books
New York
2015

This edition was produced by Blueberry Lane Books
Published in the United States of America
Cover art © Copyright 2015, Blueberry Lane Books

ISBN 978-1-942183-01-3

Blueberrylanebooks.com

TO THE MEN I SERVED WITH

CHAPTER I

This is a true story. Anyone who has served in this country's military will immediately recognize its truth. And while we don't have a St. Crispin's Day to celebrate, and our commanders were nothing like King Harry, those men who were unlucky enough not to have served will, no doubt, be doubting Thomases.

MacKenna was a rangy-built man with high cheek bones, a face composed of sharp features and very blue eyes; and like rest of us, his red hair was crew cut down to his scalp. He was a New York boy, and our unit, the 245th Infantry Battalion, was a New York National Guard unit federalized because of the Korean War and sent to Fort Bliss, Texas for training before being sent to Korea.

Even before MacKenna arrived, there was a problem. The unit was infantry, but Fort Bliss was devoted heart and soul to training artillery men. Somewhere, where decisions were made, someone had fucked up. The 245th and its entire Brigade, under the command of Colonel Sides, from Mobile, Alabama, was another "lost battalion" but in this case, it was a lost Brigade. Until such time as it was found, the men of the 245th were kept busy rearranging the rocks of the Texas landscape on Logan Heights where the unit and the rocks were located.

MacKenna, according to the 201 file was a draftee, and was officially assigned to Able Company where he wound up in my squad as a BAR (Browning automatic rifle) man. He was an expert rifleman. And though he was "easy going," he kept mostly to himself. The few friends he had were Californians, who like him were draftees. They too were "easy going" in the Californian "laid back" way. The New Yorkers, on the other hand, were "get up and go" men.

One particular Saturday morning just before standing inspection, rumor had it that our commanding officer, First Lieutenant Thomas D. Celenza was on the war path, and needed ten men for a heavy work detail. This rumor, like most of the rumors that swirled through our ranks, more than likely originated with our company clerk, Douglas Polly.

The late morning was already blazing hot, and we were in formation waiting for Celenza, who was inclined to take his time doing just about anything. A stocky man with his eyes on a Captaincy, he was always eager to show off his military stance which was why we stood inspection with fixed bayonets, sheathed of course lest one of the men accidentally cut his ear off, or playfully stick the blade into the stomach of another man.

Once inspection was over, those men who were not part of Celenza's work detail were free to go into El Paso or Juarez. Those who went into Juarez had to be back across the border by midnight. But little attention was paid to this irksome rule. Most men returned to the States via the railroad bridge over the Rio Grande that connected the two countries. Juarez was a wide open town and the many pleasures from culinary to sexual were easily available.

Celenza finally made his appearance with 1st Sergeant Carmine Valdez in tow. Valdez was new to the unit. Regular Army, he had a chest full of fruit salad from WWII and was assigned to our company as part of the cadre that would train us for combat. But so far, he was the "stranger in a strange land" in our company.

The company was called to "Attention," followed by "Shoulder Arms," then "Port Arms." Celenza began to inspect each man's piece. Show a dirty piece and you were one of the "chosen" for his detail.

When he reached MacKenna, he glanced down the barrel and declared it a dirty piece.

"Sir," MacKenna said, "would you please look at it again but with your other eye."

Celenza's jaw went slack. Valdez shook his head like a horse that has been asked to jump over a ditch and knows that if he does he will break his legs.

"Sir," MacKenna continued, "I field stripped and cleaned it less than an hour ago."

Celenza glanced at Valdez, who shrugged.

"If my piece is dirty, then it must be the fault of either the issued cleaning swabs and fluid or perhaps some defect in your right eye."

Celenza was flummoxed. "My right eye," he mumbled.

"Sir, it could be floaters, a cataract, or the beginning of detached retina."

"Are you a doctor?"

"I have two doctorates: one in Epistemology and the other in Cognitive Psychology."

Celenza had absolutely no idea what either one was, but the two -ology suffixes got to him; he inspected the rifle barrel with his left eye. After a moment or two passed, he snapped the rifle back to MacKenna and moved to the next man.

From that moment, MacKenna was given the sobriquet of Doc, and functioned in the modest capacity of "shrink" to those who needed one, and even as a scribe to those whose command of written English was seldom up to the passion felt by them, as they enlisted his service to write to their Roxannes. All of what MacKenna did was *pro bono*.

* * *

On Monday morning, Celenza ambled over to the medical detachment and had his eyes checked out by Captain Fragola, who was in the middle of his morning violin practice, and didn't take too kindly to the interruption by a hypochondriac officer. The doctor, a short chubby man, confirmed MacKenna's diagnosis: Celenza had floaters and a small cataract in his right eye.

"Nothing to worry about," Fragola said after the examination, and picking up his violin, resumed his playing.

But Celenza was a born worrier of the nail biting type. Being told not to worry was cause enough for him to worry, not only about his eye, but also about MacKenna, who, he thought, was using the army to get another high flutin' -ology doctorate.

Back at the company hutment, Celenza told Polly that he wanted "to know everything there was to know about Private MacKenna."

It was true. MacKenna had two doctoral degrees and an IQ of one hundred and fifty, which put him in the ranks of geniuses like Einstein. And it caused Celenza to have an immediate attack of *agita* and seek relief from it with an Alka-Seltzer.

"Of all the units in this man's army, why is he in this unit?" Celenza asked, putting the question to Valdez.

With a shrug of his shoulders, Valdez answered that he didn't know. Valdez' answers were seldom informational, and he wasn't much of a conversationalist. And though Polly was there during this brief exchange, he was doing what he always did between ten hundred and twelve hundred—chow time. He was zoning.

Celenza wiped his brow with a white handkerchief, grayed from too many washes. The heat was oppressive. The small, oscillating fan on his desk was overwhelmed by it and stopped moving altogether. Large blotches of sweat stained Celenza's shirt. He was a profound sweater, especially when he couldn't get his mind, so to speak, around a problem; and Private MacKenna had become his overriding problem.

* * *

While this dilemma was taking place for Celenza, a more potent one was being brewed in the office of the Battalion Commander, Lieutenant Colonel William Miller, by Master Sergeant Philip Gibbs, head of the battalion's Personnel Section, and Celenza's sworn enemy. Years before, Celenza had stolen Gibb's girl, married her and then had divorced her for a prettier woman, one with blond hair, although not a real blond according to Gibbs. Exactly how he knew that was a mystery.

Gibbs, a short, wiry built man, smoked a curved pipe, and had a gravelly, irritating voice when he barked out orders, something he was prone to do frequently whether the situation required it or not, and the situation seldom did because the section was efficiently run by Sergeant Frank Kubel and Warrant Officer John Semelinsky.

When news of the encounter between Celenza and MacKenna reached him by way of Polly, Gibbs was completely engaged by what took place between them. He too checked MacKenna's 201 File, and verified his two doctoral degrees. To be doubly sure he called the two institutions that awarded the degrees. Each required him to be transferred to several different individuals before he could authenticate the degree. The only information that bothered him in MacKenna's 201 File was the fact that the man was a qualified weapons and demolition expert even though he was a draftee. But it didn't disturb him enough to prevent two ideas to simultaneously spring to life in his brain: a man like MacKenna was wasted in a line company and belonged in Headquarters, specifically in his section; and by moving him there, it would be a way to give Celenza a zinger.

Because Gibbs and the Colonel were buddies, Gibbs had his ear whenever he wanted it. The Colonel, whose long speeches irritated the men, earned the sobriquet of Colonel Jingle Balls because his left hand was always in his pocket whenever he addressed them. He spent most of every day isolated in his office reading the daily racing forms and speaking to his newfound bookie in El Paso. He was a true pony man.

Gibbs on this particular morning introduced Private MacKenna—figuratively, of course—to the Colonel, and unequivocally stated that having MacKenna in his section would undoubtedly improve the section's performance, and that the Table of Organization and Equipment allowed for another Master Sergeant, which MacKenna, he was sure, would quickly qualify for.

The Colonel, a big man, frowned, which was what he did whenever he listened to anyone, as if the act of listening caused him pain, and it did. People took too long to tell him whatever they wanted to tell him, and there were always too many details for him to keep track of. But he was not so dense that he couldn't understand the advantage of having a man like MacKenna in Headquarters Company.

"All right, cut the order and I'll sign it," he mumbled.

Then they began to speak about baseball. Both were New York Yankee fans, and the team was in a late season slump.

Before he left the Colonel's office, Gibbs refilled his pipe and was merrily puffing on it when he returned to his desk in the personnel section.

* * *

Polly was the first man in Able Company to learn about MacKenna's impending transfer to Headquarters Company. The information came straight from Master Sergeant Gibbs, and that was the equivalent of getting it from the mountain. To score brownie points with Celenza, he immediately brought the information to his attention.

"I smell a rat," Celenza screamed and stormed off to Headquarters.

Both Polly and Valdez shook their heads and continued to do what they were previously doing, which at that time of the morning was nothing. Their expertise in that area would be hard to duplicate.

But Valdez's curiosity was aroused. He asked, in his lazy south-western drawl, "How'd ya find about it so fast Corporal?"

Polly, who looked upon Celenza and Valdez as comic characters put there by Lady Luck to relieve the tedium of army life for him, had difficulty deciding which of the two provided more laughs. And now the Lieutenant went off half-cocked to do battle with windmills; and the First Sergeant, roused out of his torpor by an event that anyone who knew anything about Celenza and Gibbs, should have seen it coming.

Imitating Valdez's drawl, Polly said, "Well, I'll tell ya, it's like this: I got real good contacts up at Battalion."

Valdez thought about what Polly said for a long while, long enough for him to remark that there was a horse fly in the hut, and it was the Corporal's duty make sure "the fly leaves or never remains alive." The choice was left up to Polly.

Having said that, Valdez lapsed into a another period of silent contemplation while Polly chased the fly around the hut, determined to swat it to a horrible death for having caused him to physically exert himself with the temperature already at a hundred degrees with noon still three hours away.

Finally the 1st Sergeant said, "Something like the Mafia, no?"

Polly paused. He was sweating profusely, as evidenced by the large dark patches on his khaki shirt. The fly also paused, happy in its fly's way not to be dodging whatever was chasing it.

Polly, who was more than slightly pissed off at Valdez and the fly, said, "Now that you put it that way, like the 'Mafia' yes."

Valdez knew all about the Mafia from the movies, and gave Polly a hard look. Polly just told him to watch his ass, and that he had friends in high places. Recognizing the possibility of danger before it actually became a danger was one of the key elements of command, and something Valdez believed he could do. So abandoning his chair, he said, "Gi'me that fuckin' fly-swatter and I'll show you how to kill a mother-fuckin' fly."

Polly smiled and gave the fly-swatter to the 1st Sergeant. From now on his life would be easier. He'd do less work than he did before and the First would do more. He loved the power of suggestion; it almost always worked.

* * *

As Lieutenant Celenza went up the steps to Headquarters, Private MacKenna went down the same steps.

"Private MacKenna," Celenza roared after returning MacKenna's smart salute, "What the fuck are you doing here?"

"Personal business with the ExO," MacKenna answered calmly.

Any questions Celenza had about MacKenna's meeting with the ExO, Major Davidson, were immediately squelched. Personal business was out of bounds.

"You didn't happen to speak to Master Sergeant Gibbs, did you?"

"No, Sir."

"So, you don't know that you're being transferred from Able Company to the Personal section of Headquarters Company."

MacKenna gave him an odd look, like—are you kidding me? Then he said, "Sir, I suggest we move off the steps to discuss this further." And at the same time he bobbed his head toward the building.

Celenza was too angry to pick up MacKenna's signal. "I'll find out soon enough if you're bullshitting me," he shouted.

MacKenna spotted Gibbs at an open window, obviously enjoying the exchange between him and

Celenza. "Sir," he said loud enough for Celenza and Gibbs to hear, "We're being watched and overheard."

Celenza got the message, glared at Gibbs, and as he turned, the flush on his face deepened until it was almost purple. But he followed MacKenna until they were a couple of dozen paces away from Headquarters.

"If I find out that you've bullshitted me, your ass is grass," Celenza threatened.

Still speaking calmly, MacKenna answered, "I don't want a transfer. I am perfectly happy where I am."

"The Army doesn't give a flying fuck if you're happy, or if you're not happy," Clenza growled.

"Sir, perhaps I used the wrong word to describe my psychological state. But I'm sure you know what I mean.

Celenza's anger was beginning to cool.

"Sir, you know you can't win this one now," MacKenna said, "so why don't we go back to the company area and discuss the situation."

Celenza was about to object when MacKenna said, "Remember Falstaff's words—"

"Who the fuck is he?"

"Sir, let's leave that for another time," MacKenna answered.

"Yah," Celenza agreed and began to walk toward the company area.

* * *

A war council was held by Celenza. He sat behind his desk while the 1st and the Corporal sat behind their desks. Private MacKenna was left standing with his back to the door. Though the hutment was stifling hot, he was happy to be out of the blistering heat and almost blinding glare of the sun.

Celenza had Polly phone the Mess and order two pitchers of ice water, and the four of them drank copiously before Celenza opened the discussion by stating the problem confronting them—how to hold on to MacKenna.

The discussion went on for an hour. MacKenna seldom spoke. Most of what was said was said between Celenza and Polly. The 1st wanted no part in any scheme that would cross Gibbs and the Colonel. But it was obvious to MacKenna that Polly liked the game, and it was even more obvious when the Corporal said, "There are a couple of things we could do that would confuse the shit out of Gibbs and the Colonel."

Like the snap of a whip, Valdez stood and said, "Soldier you're out of line. They wear the uniform and have the rank."

"I meant no disrespect, Sergeant," Polly wheedled.

"I think we know what Corporal Polly meant," Celenza said.

"Thank you, Sir," Polly responded.

"Could you be a little more explicit, Corporal?" MacKenna asked, entering the conversation after a long silence.

Celenza and his two non-coms looked at him with obvious surprise. Though the discussion was about him, they almost forgot that he was there all the time.

"Sir," MacKenna said, "I request permission to sit."

Celenza looked confused.

"A chair, Sir," MacKenna explained. "My legs hurt."

"Ah, yes. A chair!" Celenza said, and motioned him to the chair in front of his desk.

Polly waited until MacKenna was seated before he said, "Our TOE calls for a Sergeant First Class for the machine gun section, and—"

Celenza interrupted him. "You're a weapons man MacKenna, aren't you?"

"Yes, Sir."

Celenza turned his attention to Polly.

"Sir, if you promote Private MacKenna that would make him a weapons section chief."

MacKenna wanted to smile, but forced himself not to. Things were going his way, while Polly was scoring "brownie points" with the Lieutenant, lots of them.

"What will that do?" Valdez asked, piqued by Polly's suggestion. It took him years to make Sergeant and many more years to become a First Sergeant. For a draftee to move to the exalted rank of Platoon Sergeant was something he had never seen in his twenty years of service, and it stuck in his craw.

"It will put him out of Gibb's reach. The Regs say that when it comes to filling the TOE requirements of a line company, its needs supersede any other, including those of a Headquarters Section."

"But what about—"

"The transfer order?"

Celenza nodded. "I'm sure it's been cut."

"Lost. Mislaid," Polly offered. "And found again at the proper time."

"It ain't legal, Sir," Valdez barked.

Celenza gave him a quizzical look. "It's legal if you can get away with it."

And Polly added enthusiastically, "And I think we can get away with it, Sir, for twenty four hours; and by that time MacKenna will be a Sergeant First Class, and our new weapons section chief."

Valdez grimaced; he didn't want to cross Celenza, who could make his life miserable, and he didn't want to do anything that might cause him to be court-martialed.

Valdez's silence was too long for Celenza, and he ordered Polly to, "Do it. Get it done."

CHAPTER II

Celenza, Carmine, and MacKenna vacated the hut, leaving Polly alone to do the necessary paper work to promote MacKenna to Sergeant First Class. Polly was especially pleased with the outcome of the meeting. He liked the games he was playing. Intrigue and finance were his specialties. The financial angle came from the money lending operation that he and Gibbs set up. They charged the usual two for five, with vigor, increasing by two dollars for every delinquent month if the client failed to pay up at the end of the month when, in the parlance of the men, "The eagle shits."

His financial activities made him the friend of many of the men in and out of the company enabling him to build a network of men who were more than willing to do favors for him, little things like slipping a predated company order into a pile of orders that Gibbs seldom read before they reached the Colonel for his signature. He was too occupied with his bookie to read everything that required his signature.

What escalated Polly's enjoyment of the situation he created was his duplicity; he was "burning both ends of the candle." Gibbs was his "big daddy," bankrolling their financial enterprise and splitting the profits equally. But there seemed to be another "friend" in the company, and the evidence pointed to MacKenna, who always had a full wallet, and in the short time he'd been in the company had gained the reputation for being a generous person. Polly simultaneously saw him as a potential threat to his business activities, or a possible partner, which was why he wanted MacKenna to remain in the company where he could "keep an eye on him." When the opportunity came, and he was sure it would come, he would talk business with him.

* * *

It was Carmine's sad task to introduce Acting Sergeant First Class James MacKenna to Sergeant Vincent Trappaso, and explain to him that he was no longer the Acting Section Chief of the Heavy Weapons Section. The two walked leisurely to where Trappaso and his men were, which was where all of the battalion's Heavy Weapons Sections were located, the near side of a huge drainage ditch that formed the dividing line between Federal and private property— The Open Eye Ranch—and the two rancher's daughters were indeed full-breasted, long-legged eye openers making it difficult for the men to concentrate on their 50s.

On the way there, Carmine, not at all happy with what took place a short while before in the Company's Orderly Room, offered the comment, "This is the goddamnedest outfit I've ever been in."

"How so?" MacKenna questioned.

"First, you got the New York boys who get things done yesterday; then, you got the California bunch, who thinks *mañana* is just too fast. And that's just for openers."

"You're RA, aren't you?"

"Damn right I am and I go by the fuckin' book," Carmine said proudly. "But these bastards have their own fuckin' book, an' it ain't anythin' like the Army's."

Nothing more was said by either of them until Carmine stopped, and said, "Trappaso is Celenza's cousin on his mother's side. Almost all of the wops are in the Company are related to each other or are friends of each other's family."

"What about the other men, excluding those from California?"

"A few Hebs, Micks an' Bohunks for good measure."

They continued to walk and Carmine said, "Trappaso ain't goin' to it like this, and I don't like it. It ain't by the book."

"That's one of the many things about the army that's different from civilian life. You have to do things that you don't like to do," MacKenna said.

Carmine gave him a quick look. Then he said, "That's for fuckin' sure."

The walk from the Orderly Room to where the Heavy Weapons Section was located was all uphill, and by the time they reached it, their fatigues were blotched with sweat front and back.

Trappaso, a short, chubby man, was standing in the center of a circle formed by the men in the section. With Trappaso, spread out on a shelter half, was a disassembled .50 caliber machine gun, and in his hand was service manual, TM-50, that provided detailed instructions on the operation, troubleshooting and repair of the weapon. Having disassembled it, which was easy, he now faced the task of reassembling it into its former operating condition. And that became a problem for him. As a garbage man in civilian life for his uncle on his father's side, who ran a garbage collecting business in Brooklyn, he hadn't any need to read beyond the sports pages of the Daily News, where only the scores interested him and not the writings of the sports columnists.

Seeing Carmine and MacKenna approach provided a welcome reason to give his men a ten minute break.

Carmine didn't waste words.

"Sergeant MacKenna is the new acting Section Chief."

Trappaso looked at MacKenna, then at Carmine. His lips moved, but he said nothing until he cleared his throat and in a squeaky voice said, "Since when?"

"The Lieutenant is probably signing the orders just about now," Carmine answered.

"Fuckin' son-of-a-bitch!" Trappaso exploded. "Wait 'till Angie finds out. All fuckin' hell is goin' to break fuckin' loose."

MacKenna leaned close to Carmine. "Who's Angie?"

Carmine shrugged. "His wife, I guess."

Trappaso threw the TM on the ground, and let loose a burst of Italian.

MacKenna stepped toward him. "Pick up the TM and give it to me," he said, his voice flat with threatening danger.

Trappaso didn't move.

"That's an order, soldier," MacKenna said.

Carmine was mystified by what he saw was happening.

"Pick it up," MacKenna ordered.

Reluctantly Trappaso obeyed and handed the TM to MacKenna, who said, "You put a curse on me. Next time you do that, I'll have you busted down to a Private, *capisce*?"

"You speak Italian?" Carmine asked.

"Italian, French, Spanish and German," MacKenna answered.

"Holy shit!" Carmine exclaimed.

"That's about right," MacKenna answered. "Now let's assemble the fucking 50."

* * *

Carmine left MacKenna with the Heavy Weapon's Section, and walked slowly back to the Company Orderly Room. Something didn't click. The MacKenna he just saw wasn't the same MacKenna he had known. They looked the same, but didn't act the same and certainly didn't speak the same.

Suddenly, he stopped. The new MacKenna was Army—Army all the way—no bullshit. The son-of-a-bitch isn't—Wait, he's a fuckin' plant. They goddamn planted him on us. He struck his forehead with the palm of his right hand.

"Okay," he said aloud. "Okay, just play it straight and see where it goes. Keep what you saw buttoned-up."

He continued to walk. "One thing is for sure, MacKenna ain't goin' to let anyone piss on him, Angie or no Angie."

* * *

With the paperwork finished, and Celenza's and Carmine's signatures on all the required forms needed to promote MacKenna to Sergeant First Class and Section Chief of the Heavy Weapons Section, Polly leisurely walked to Battalion Headquarters; and as he walked, he reversed the position of his watch, so that the stem was opposite his wrist.

His first stop in Headquarters was the Message Center, where his friend, Sergeant John Santana worked.

"Get these papers to the Colonel, ASAP," he said. "Very important for the war effort."

Santana glanced at the papers and gave Polly a hard look. "I got paper from Gibbs sayin' he's been transferred to—"

Polly's right hand came up. "Mine come first. His gets lost for a couple of days."

"Shit," Santana growled.

"Next loan is free," Polly said.

"It's a big fuckin' risk. If Gibbs finds out, my ass is grass."

Polly knew that this time Santana held all the cards.

"One for five thereafter," Polly offered.

"Five gets five," Santana countered.

"Next thing, I'll be paying you," Polly said sourly.

Santana guffawed.

Polly didn't think the remark was even worth a smile, and meandered over to the Personnel Section where he chatted with a couple of the men before he made his way to Gibbs' desk.

The Sergeant immediately noticed that Polly's watch was upside down, and it gave him an uneasy feeling. Though he and Polly were partners, he didn't completely trust Polly, and he was sure Polly felt the same way about him.

They exchanged greetings; then Gibbs said, "Corporal your watch is upside down."

"Ah so it is, Sergeant," Polly answered. "I wouldn't have noticed it."

"Nothing pressing?"

Polly's eyes twinkled.

Gibbs never liked it when Polly's eyes twinkled. It meant that Polly was enjoying the situation. He felt safer when the Corporal's eyes were their usual dull gray.

"Business as usual," Polly said leaving Gibbs even more uneasy than when he saw that Polly's watch was upside down.

* * *

One of the telephone lines from Logan Heights to El Paso hummed with Trappaso reciting his demotion from Acting Section Chief to an ordinary Sergeant, and Angie on the other end of the line became angrier and angrier—so angry that she threatened to confront Celenza herself, and remind him that family is family.

Trappaso didn't think that was a good idea.

"Okay, I won't do it, but I'm going to call my father, and he'll call Uncle Leo, and you know Uncle Leo ain't goin' to like this one goddam bit. He'll call

Celenza an' get everythin' straightened out. You just sit tight."

"Yeah, and this MacKenna guy understands Italian, and a few other languages as well."

"How do you know that?"

"I put a curse on him in Italian, and he understood it."

"What kind of curse?"

"That his balls and dick shrivel up and fall off."

"You said that?"

"In Italian."

"Holy shit!"

"I didn't say that one," Trappaso answered.

"Don't worry about it, honey. Uncle Leo will fix it."

"I sure hope so," Trappaso said sadly.

"He will. He will. A million kisses. I'll see you tonight," Angie said and clicked off.

Trappaso left the phone booth. He wasn't at all reassured by what Angie had told him. Having been in the army during World War II, Trappaso doubted that Angie's Uncle Leo's influence extended into the army. He was in the army again because Celenza talked him into joining the National Guard, which wasn't a bad deal at all. Everyone knew everyone else. It was a big club and you got paid for joining; you got two weeks more vacation to go on summer maneuvers. A month after he joined, Celenza promoted him to Sergeant. That was five years ago, and now a snot-nose draftee comes and fucks up his chances for promotion. He knew that some guys were lucky and some weren't. He was one of the unlucky ones; he was sure of that.

* * *

It wasn't until Celenza returned home that he gave any thought to Vinny. After the meeting in the Company Orderly Room, he spent the rest of the afternoon in the motor-pool bullshitting with Captain Ronald Verhey about MacKenna. Verhey didn't like either Gibbs or the Colonel. For his money, Gibbs was a card shark, who was more noise than substance. As for the Colonel, he couldn't fight his way out of a paper bag unless his bookie was with him.

But Celenza and Verhey had much in common. Verhey, like him had been in WWII, and had become officers in the Guard. In civilian life, Celenza had worked in his father's paint store, while Verhey had worked in his uncle's real-estate office Neither one had been happy with what they had been doing. Then the situation in Korea had suddenly blossomed into a war. As a result, they had been transformed into what they now were—officers in the United States Army. Both saw that as almost a God-given gift. Of the two, Verhey was the better business man, and to prove it to anyone who might have asked, he would tell them that he took a flyer with whatever savings he had and bought ten thousand khaki shirts that the army surplus had auctioned off at a dollar a shirt. Three days after the Korean War had begun, he sold them back to the Army at twelve dollars a shirt. Because this transaction was common knowledge among the officers and enlisted men of Headquarters Company, Verhey was considered a financial wizard. Celenza was sure that some of Verhey's wizardry would somehow migrate to him, and enable him to also make a killing.

But all of Celenza's good feelings vanished as soon as he arrived home, and Silvia said, "What the hell did you do to Vinny?"

"Vinny?"

"Angie called her father, and he's going to call Leo," Silvia said.

In his rush to secure MacKenna, he had completely forgotten about Vinny.

"The shit has really hit the fan," Silvia told him.

"Listen, the army is army," he answered hoping that would silence her though he knew it wouldn't— Vinny was her cousin—family.

"What are you going to do about it?

"Right now, nothing," he said. "Right now, I want to have my dinner, play with the kids and—"

The phone rang.

"Uncle Leo, I bet," she said.

He picked it up. "Lieutenant Celenza, here," he said.

The man on the other end spoke in Italian. *"Listen, I bust your fuckin' head open if you don't give Vinny back his job. He's family, remember that. You hear me?*

In English, Celenza said, "No can do."

"I say you do."

"Leo, you can't tell the Army what to do."

"No shit, but I can tell you what to do."

"Leo, Vinny is lucky he's where he is," Celenza said. "Now you just go about your business and I'll go about mine. I have an infantry company to run and you..."

"You brushing me off?"

"I'm just telling it to you like it is," Celenza answered, and put the phone down.

Wide eyed, Silvia stared at him. "Are nuts you, or something? That was Leo you just told off."

"Yeah, so what?" Celenza asked.

"Vinny—"

"I got a new Section Chief, and that's that," Celenza said. "Now I'd like my dinner."

"That's all you're getting, if you know what I mean," she said, and flounced into the kitchen.

Celenza raised his eyes, and silently asked, "Why me? Why me?"

* * *

Twenty minutes later, Celenza's father, George, phoned. He too spoke in Italian, and said, *"Leo is very sad and angry, and when he's that way he goes to church to pray for guidance, and when he comes out, he's Leo the Tiger. And that's not good."*

"Pop, he can come out Leo the Gorilla, but that wouldn't change things. My new Section Chief is a fucking genius; and you know Vinny is dumb as shit."

"He's family."

"That don't make him smart," Celenza said.

"Leo is a big man."

"In Bensonhurst and Dyker Beach, but not here in El Paso and Fort Bliss. Pop, the Army doesn't give a rat's ass for Leo's bigness because the army's so big that guys like Leo are smaller than mosquitoes to it."

"You make me feel ashamed."

Suddenly an idea came to Celenza. "Listen, Pop, I don't want you to tell this to anyone, but the new Section Chief is part of a secret mission. Understand, Pop. I can't talk about it. But Vinny will have to live with it. It's big stuff, a big secret."

"No shit?"

"As God is my judge, no shit."

His father was satisfied, and the said "good night" to each other.

"Secret?" Silvia asked.

Celenza nodded and said, "I can't tell you anything about it, but I saved Vinny's balls."

"Saved his balls?"

"Yeah, but let it go at that," Celenza said, pleased with his inventiveness. "Angie wouldn't have much of a husband if wasn't for me."

"Why didn't you say so in the first place?"

"Because, Silvia, it's a secret," Celenza answered. "You already know too much; so keep your mouth shut. Not a word to Angie. Understand?

She nodded.

Celenza nodded, but didn't believe her nod. The secret would be all over the battalion in a day or two at the most.

* * *

MacKenna sat at the table in the far corner of the Queen Bee, a combination ice-cream parlor and hamburger joint located on the highway between Logan Heights and the military airport that serviced Fort Bliss. The place was crowded and noisy, but for some odd reason most of the men preferred to stand at the counter. Most of them were from the 245th, and like him skipped chow and opted for food and drink more comforting than army fare. He was happily enjoying a chocolate ice-cream soda, and thinking about the events of the day. With the exception of his encounter with Trappaso, he was pleased with the way they went. Trappaso would sulk for a few days, but because he was in the army, he hadn't any choice other than to live with his loss. Besides, sooner or later, he'd prove himself unequal to the responsibility of being a Section Chief.

He was thinking of going up to the counter and ordering a cheeseburger when he saw Polly enter and walk to the rear where there was an empty table for two. Though he could see Polly from where he was, Polly couldn't see him. Polly being there didn't strike him as strange, but the fact that Polly hadn't ordered anything to eat or drink did strike him as odd and aroused his curiosity. Without food or drink in front of him, he guessed that Polly must be waiting for someone, maybe a woman.

Five minutes after Polly entered the Queen Bee; Gibbs arrived and went straight to where Polly was seated. Their meeting was obviously prearranged. The two were hiding, so to speak, in plain sight. They began a conversation. The expression on Gibbs' face never changed. Polly smiled a lot, and laughed a couple of times.

MacKenna was certain that Polly was playing Gibbs about something, the way he'd seen him play Celenza earlier. Now and then Gibbs' face flushed. Their meeting lasted twenty minutes. Neither shook the other's hand. Gibbs left first. Polly immediately followed. And for the tenth time, "Goodnight Irene, Goodnight" poured out of the juke box.

* * *

Polly went back to the Battalion area, and caught the next bus for El Paso where he would cross into Mexico and the city of Juarez. The bus ride took thirty minutes, and because he went to the last stop, he was a block away from the International Bridge. A Border Patrol guard at the bridge reminded him that he had to be back across the bridge in Texas by midnight. He saluted the guard, acknowledging the warning, and crossed the Rio Grande that, because of a two year drought, looked more like a dry gulch than a river bed.

In Juarez, Polly went to Manelos, a brothel that became the unofficial Headquarters for the 245th Infantry Battalion. Rita, his favorite girl, was at the bar drinking tea from a shot glass that the man she was with paid for as if it was Scotch or Rye, or whatever her client ordered. The bar was crowded. The room was noisy and full of smoke. Business was good. The guy she was with was either a tourist or a local from El Paso out for an evening of booze and sex.

When she saw Polly, she flashed him a big smile.

He nodded to her.

The guy she was with, Phil, looked at Polly and asked, "You know him?"

"A little bit," she answered.

Phil pursed his lips. He knew her "little bit" meant a whole lot, and he didn't want any competition. Rita was a looker with long black hair and black eyes that flashed with laughter; she couldn't have been more than eighteen or twenty at the most. She had a body, most of which he could see, that filled his imagination with visions of delight the way the coming of Christmas makes a kid think of the toys he'll get. He desperately wanted her to be his toy.

"How much for the whole night?" he asked.

"No can do," Rita said.

He frowned. "A hundred bucks, US."

She shook her head.

"Two hundred," Phil offered.

"I'll fuck you, ten dollars, then goodbye," she said.

Suddenly he grabbed hold of her shoulders. "I want you—"

From the bar, Polly saw that and signaled to two of his friends. The three of them quickly surrounded Phil and Rita.

"She's coming with me," Polly said, taking hold of one of her hands.

"What's going on here?" Phil questioned.

"Hey, guys, is anything going on here?"

His two friends looked around, and one said, "Nope. Nothin's happenin'."

"Better leave," Polly said, "before something does happen."

"You squirt, are you threatening me?"

Phil put his hand is his jacket pocket, but before he could remove it, his face was slashed and he was rabbit-punched at the back of his neck, which knocked him to the floor.

Polly put his hand into the man's jacket pocket and pulled out a .32 caliber silver-colored automatic with faux pearl handle, "A lady's gun," he said and stuck it in his belt under his shirt. "Okay, strip him to his underwear, and leave him where the police or Federales will find him."

His friends followed his instructions and dragged Phil out into the alley, while he and Rita, hand in hand, walked up the steps to her room, where the writhing body of Christ on the cross that decorated the otherwise bare wall looked down on their writhing bodies in bed with blind eyes and deaf ears to their cries of ecstasy.

* * *

The next afternoon Silvia and Angie met for lunch in Frank's Trattoria, across the street from the El Paso Del Norte, the best hotel in El Paso. Silvia had phoned Angie early that morning and told her she had something, very, very, very important to tell her.

Both women were beautiful and stylishly dressed. They occupied a booth across from the bar where the men could see them in the mirror behind the bar and they could see the men. Not that they were interested in making a connection, but both enjoyed being admired and silently played the game of what if with any attractive man who seemed interested in them.

The only thing Italian about Frank's Trattoria was its name. Most of the food described on the menu was Mexican, and the spaghetti sauce, they learned from a prior luncheon, was catsup. Both of them settled for a

Mexican omelet, which was a variation of a Spanish omelet but spicier, and iced tea.

With their order out of the way, Silvia said, "What I'm going to tell you is hush-hush—top secret really."

Angie responded with a nod, and the man in the booth behind theirs also nodded.

"First, not to worry," Silvia said, "Tom will switch Vinny to Supplies, where he'll be able to get his promotion."

"Oh that's wonderful!" Angie responded.

"Tom wanted Vinny out of the way because of the new ammunition," Silvia said.

The man in the booth took out a reporter's notebook and a pen, and jotted down, "new ammunition."

"It's like this," Silvia said, "every fourth round is ordinarily a tracer, now the new one will have a smidgen of nuclear stuff that can go through three feet of armor plate and out the other side, like say a tank; then the tank collapses because the round sucks out all of the air in it as it goes out the other side. And if it hits a man, he's gone. Poof. Up in smoke, vaporized."

The reporter got everything Silvia said, in shorthand.

"See," Silvia continued, "Vinny would have been handling hot ammunition. And any leaks would have affected his balls."

"His balls," Angie repeated in alarm.

Silvia crossed her lips with her forefinger.

"Sorry, "Angie whispered.

"The new guy in the section is some sort of genius, a nuclear specialist."

"Wow!"

"Yeah, that's what I said, when he told me," Silvia said

The waitress brought their orders to the table; and when she left, Angie asked, "How did you get Tom to tell you?"

Silvia laughed. "It was easy; I gave him a really fancy blow job. He loves that."

The reporter snickered, but not loudly. He had a scoop that would make him look good, very good.

CHAPTER III

That night after dinner when their two children, Peter and Melinda, were asleep, Tom and Silvia listened to music coming from XELO, a station whose broadcasting area dominated much of southwestern Texas, New Mexico and part of Arizona. Neither one of them paid any attention to the music that served as background for their time together.

Tom was particularly pleased with the way the day went. He checked out the Heavy Weapons section and saw that Mac Kenna had everything under control. The men listened to him and responded to his questions. He was a natural leader, and later in the day, MacKenna had the men doing close order drill while happily calling out Jodi Choruses. Even Vinney fell into the rhythm of the march.

There was a meeting at Headquarters during which the Colonel, boring as usual, told the assembled officers to prepare their men for their first field exercise that would begin the following Monday and take place in the desert, forty miles northeast of Logan Heights. Detailed information would be sent to each Company Commander by the Operations Section. That having been said, they were dismissed. But most of them lingered awhile in groups of two, three and even five, where they discussed the coming mission. The group of five held the opinion that such an exercise was at least a month or six weeks premature. The men weren't ready for a tactical exercise. Tom didn't offer any judgment one way or another.

After the group split up, he went to the Company Orderly Room to see if anything needed his attention.

Carmine reported that "everything was under control."

Polly handed him the necessary papers to sign that would move Vinny to Supplies with the comment, "Corporal Strumph isn't going to be happy when Vinny comes marching in."

"So what am I supposed to do about that?" Celenza asked while signing the papers.

"I'll give that some thought," Polly replied.

Celenza gave him a quick look, but didn't say anything and left the orderly room to spend the rest of the day in the Motor Pool with Verhey.

These were the thoughts that floated through Tom's mind, though not in any particular order. It had been a good day, and he was thinking about going to bed. The Colonel insisted all Company Commanders had to be present for the five-thirty A.M. roll call, something none of them enjoyed doing.

He was about to leave the couch when Silvia said, "The weirdest thing happened at lunch this afternoon."

"Oh!"

"I was with Angie."

"And you told her about Vinny," he said.

"I had to," said Silvia. "She was—"

"Never mind how she was, just tell me what you want to tell me. I'm tired and—"

"This guy picked up our tab, and sent two drinks to us," she said.

Tom squinted at her. "Why?"

She shrugged.

"He's after one of your pussies or both of them," he said.

"We don't even know who it was."

"What do you mean?"

"We never saw him."

"And the barkeep didn't identify him?"

"He only said it was the man in the booth behind ours," she said.

Tom scratched his head and with a shrug told him she was going to bed. "You coming?"

"How could I refuse an invitation like that?"

He stood, reached down and pulled her up off the couch. "Like last night," he said. This would be a good end to a good day.

"Then, like last night," Silvia said

They laughed.

* * *

Tom and Silvia were frenching it. She was on top of him facing his feet and he was beneath her devouring her vagina. In the course of this uninhibited activity, Silvia's imagination aided by the pleasure Tom so avidly gave her, kicked in and in its unique way added spice to what was quickly becoming orgasmic. She thought about the mystery man who picked up the tab and sent two additional drinks to the table. What did he look like? Was he sexy? Would he go for oral sex or was he strictly the missionary position type? Married to Tom for five years she'd never really thought about having a different man in bed with her. But now as she began to softly moan with pleasure and Tom also began to utter sounds of delight as she used her tongue and lips on his cock, she couldn't stop thinking about doing what she was doing with Tom with the mystery man. And the very next instant she let loose a wordless cry of orgasmic ecstasy and Tom came immediately afterward with an enormous growl of satisfaction.

Later, when they felt the calmness and the ting of depression that follows such emotional and physical exertion, she asked Tom if he ever thought of doing what that they had done with another woman.

"Not since we began doing it," he answered. "Why should I think about doing with someone else when you're great?"

She appreciatively patted his cock, but didn't pursue the subject with him, though silently she did purse it and made up her mind to find out the name of the mysterious man. She was sure that the waiter knew him. A five buck tip might do the trick. She smiled, wrapped her right arm around Tom's chest and drifted into a lovely, deep sleep.

* * *

F.K. Pulp, a sparsely built man, with a pepper-salt colored mustache, and wearing a white-ten gallon hat and black snake skin boots, dropped four sheets of double spaced copy on the editor's desk at the *El Paso Herald* a few hours after he left the restaurant.

The editor, Luke Short, squinted up at him, and asked, "Won't go until the morning edition."

"Put it on the wire and watch the fireworks," Pulp said, biting off the end of the cigar and depositing it in an ashtray on Short's desk. "But first read it."

Short scanned the copy. "Holy goddamn shit. it's fucking dynamite. Where'd you get the info?"

Pulp lit his cigar and waving it front of Short said, "A secret source of information."

Short who always looked like a bull dog looked even more like one.

"Get it on the wire," Pulp said.

"Will there be any follow ups?" Short asked.

Pulp shrugged. "Only the gods know that," he said, with the cigar already on the right side of his mouth.

Short left his desk and went over to where the teletype machine was, looked back at Pulp for a moment, and then began typing. Within five minutes after he signed off, every phone in the office rang.

"What'd I tell you," Pulp said, blowing a couple of smoke rings.

* * *

Tom's sleep, usually blissful after having sex, wasn't at all blissful. Filled with wild dreams that included Gibbs and MacKenna, Polly and Carmine and people he didn't even know pointing their accusing fingers at him. One particular sequence disturbed him so much, it actually woke him ... He was running up a hill and each time he reached the top, the hill suddenly got higher ... Jerking awake, he realized he was sweating. He checked the time on the alarm clock. It was four o'clock; in another half hour, he'd have to get up anyway. That fact had eliminated any idea of him going back to sleep. He left the bed, padded into the living room and sat in club chair thinking about that dream that woke him.

* * *

By the dawn's early light, the War Department, the Federal Bureau of Investigation and the Commanding General, Major General James Gunner the Third, had been alerted to the fact that the wire story out of El Paso, Texas, while not stating an actual truth, had come too damn close for comfort. The Army was indeed experimenting with nuclear artillery rounds that could pierce a tank's armor and in exiting, the tank would collapse, as it was stated in the wire story.

J. Edgar Hoover immediately detailed fifty agents to El Paso to seek out the Red Menace, while General Gunner, also a big fan of the Red Menace Club, called a staff meeting and detailed his aide, Brigadier William Shot, to begin an investigation of every enlisted man and officer in Fort Bliss, and there were eighty-two thousands of them. General Shot, in turn, ordered his aide, Colonel Donald Bomb, to run checks on all of the civilian workers on the base.

While these very big wheels were turning, Celenza saw the front page story immediately after roll call. He was at his desk when he opened the paper, and let loose with, "Holy fucking shit and it's in the newspaper. It's in the fucking newspaper."

Neither Polly nor Carmine who were at their desks knew what he was talking about.

"There's a goddamn story here," said Celenza, trying to cover his initial outburst, "that says we got Reds on the base."

"Reds?" Polly questioned.

"Commies."

"Like Russians—" Carmine began

"Commies, for God's sake," Celenza said. "How do I know whether they're Russian, Chinese, or just plain Americans?"

At that point in the conversation, the phone rang and Celenza was summoned to an emergency staff meeting, ASAP.

His first thought before leaving was to take the newspaper with him, but that he quickly realized would look too peculiar, especially to Polly, who d be quick to pick up on something like that. Instead, he left it on his desk and practically ran out of the office and up to Headquarters.

As soon as the door closed, Polly went for the paper, quickly scanned the story and said to Carmine, "You're not going to believe this," and he read the story to Carmine, who, after Polly finished, let go with a long whistle, followed by, "There just ain't any damn thing like tracers with nuclear tips. The guy who wrote that don't know shit from shinola about fifty caliber ammo."

Polly looked quizzically at Carmine.

"Can't trust what's in the newspapers," the First Sergeant said.

Polly was going to say, *you're right*, but instead, he said nothing. The proverbial fat was in the frying pan, and Celenza was the fat. He was sure that MacKenna would know that too once he read the story, and Gibbs was certain to make the connection between Celenza and the story. The big question, of course, was how the story got to be the story, and then got to F.K. Pulp, the guy who wrote it.

Even as Polly thought about the news story, he idly turned the pages of the newspaper; then he stopped. There was a photograph identifying the man his friends had beaten up, stripped and dropped in the alleyway for the police or the Federales to find. The man was Philip Trees, the middle son of Honest Jack Trees, a prominent oil man and a possible candidate for the U.S. Senate, and possibly the Presidency afterwards. All of the excitement of the last few minutes dwindled to nothing. Phil Trees swore to find the man who humiliated him and his family and in no uncertain terms, he said, "When I get that son-of-a-bitch, I'm going to give him a lesson in Texas style justice, one he'll never forget." That was enough to put a damper on Polly's day; he was in danger of being hurt, badly hurt, and he was frightened.

* * *

The meeting at Headquarters was restricted to Officers and Warrant Officers, and because of the clubby nature of the federalized National Guard Unit, all of them knew each other, and had known each other for years. A few had served together in the same unit during WWII.

The Colonel, who got the word from Colonel Sides, the Brigade Commander, was not sure what he was supposed to do. Since the story was already in the newspaper there wasn't any way to take it out of the newspaper. But to be on the safe side, he read the story out loud so that every one of the Officers and Warrant Officers understood that the story had upset the command all the way up to the War Department and all the way back down to the battalion level. He had not been informed that the FBI was involved and would soon be a very visible presence, nor was he told about the massive investigations ordered by Major General James Gunner.

So for a few minutes after the story was read, no one said a word; Celenza was sweating a lot more than he usually did. He no longer had any fingernails to chew on and chewing on the tips of his fingers would just attract attention to him, which was something he didn't need. He had made the whole thing up to keep Silvia off his back about Trappaso. Somewhere he'd read about nuclear tipped artillery shells and what they could do. But that story was in in a Science-Fiction magazine. He used it because he remembered it. That Silvia repeated the story to Angie he figured would happen, but he didn't figure on a reporter hearing it too.

Suddenly, the Colonel announced, 'I want every one of you to keep your eyes and ears open. The Red Menace is very real. This meeting is adjoined."

* * *

Both Mac Kenna and Gibbs suspected where the story came from, but could not prove it. Gibbs felt that if Celenza had finally fallen into deep shit, that wasn't his problem. He'd let other people worry about it. He had his own problem with Celenza, and that was what interested him more than nuclear tipped fifty caliber tracer rounds.

As for MacKenna's take on the news story, he too couldn't have cared less. He had his section to whip into shape for the coming maneuvers, and he had one or two odds and ends, as he privately referred to them, to take care of. But as he always did, he wrote an account of events of the day in a small copy book using a combination of Latin, Ancient Greek and modern French and German. This combination of languages insured security, a necessary precaution.

Celenza and Verhey left headquarters together, but stopped a short distance from it to discuss the events of the non-meeting. Celenza, at least, for the immediate present felt relieved that no fingers had been pointed at him and Verhey felt that the Colonel had been at his most ineffective.

"The trouble with the Colonel," Verhey said, "is that he is like a fart in a windstorm. If I were in his shoes, I would have immediately appointed three officers to investigate the matter."

Celenza hadn't any choice but to agree with a silent nod.

"He's leaving all of it to Brigade and higher," Verhey said.

"Maybe he doesn't want to rock the boat," Celenza offered. "He has enough trouble with Brigade as it."

"Yeah, it's the Civil War all over again. Brigade is from Mobile, Alabama and we're from New York," he said shaking his head.

"Well, I better get back to the Orderly Room and see what's going on there," Celenza said.

They nodded to each other and went their separate ways: Verhey to the Motor Pool and Celenza to the Company Orderly Room, where he found the morning newspaper just where he left it on his desk and Polly and Carmine at their respective desks. For several moments he rescanned the story, sighed loudly, and realized he was a knife's edge away from being in very big trouble. His dream of getting his "railroad tracks" had since he first read the story all but faded into another one of his disappointments. But this time, it was Silvia's big mouth that sunk his ship.

Suddenly he realized that the Orderly Room was absolutely quiet. He looked at Carmine. The First Sargent's eyes were closed; he was probably into a catnap. But Polly, who no doubt had read the newspaper while he was at Headquarters, looked absolutely woebegone; and was silent, a rarity for him.

Despite his own unhappy predicament, Celenza was concerned about what he perceived as Polly being unlike Polly, and for the very selfish reason that he could always count on Polly more than Carmine to make it easy for him to run the Company, he didn't want anything untoward to happen to him. But for him to have asked Polly if anything was wrong or if he felt ill would have been a breach of military protocol, something he felt he couldn't risk doing in his unsettled condition. Besides, he had enough problems of his own to deal with; he didn't need someone else's baggage as well.

* * *

By nine-thirty in the morning, Silvia and Angie were on the phone. Both had read the newspaper story and had heard it on the radio. And both of them were filled with the delicious excitement that came from being in the center of a whirlwind and knowing that only Tom knew that they were the origin of story. Vinny didn't know that because he only read the sports section. Besides, he wouldn't have given a "rat's ass" about it because he was still fuming about his demotion and the orders transferring him to Supply hadn't come through as yet.

Both women were in their nightgowns with a light house dress over them. Neither one understood the gravity of the situation: that in some strange way they had breached a vital security chain.

"So the guy's name is F.K. Pulp," Silvia said.

"Do you think that's his real name?" Angie asked.

Though Angie couldn't see her, Silvia said with a shrug, "I'll find out later this afternoon."

"Are you going to the newspaper?"

"Back to the restaurant," Silvia said and paused a moment before she asked, "Wanna come with me?"

For a moment or two, Angie remained silent, but it was long enough for Silvia to say, "It just might be some fun. You know a kind of innocent flirtation. Happens all the time."

Angie giggled.

"Is that a yes or a no?"

"Absolutely, a yes," Angie said.

"Good, I'll pick you up at twelve-thirty," Silvia told her

"Wow! I never thought, I'd have the nerve to do something like this," Angie said.

"Me neither," Silvia answered and clicked off.

CHAPTER IV

The meeting was held in Ramblin' Rose's office, the owner and publisher of the El Paso Times. Ramblin' came by that name when he was a much younger man, gaining a reputation for rambling with other men's wives and sweethearts. But now nature and late marriage to a physically demanding woman a quarter of a century younger than him, had changed his rambling ways, and made him into a church-going docile creature. His office was all mahogany and he was having his usual breakfast of flapjacks, three sausages, coffee and a shot of Wild Turkey.

Ramblin', as he preferred to be called—either with the Mister before it or without it, if it was a friend addressing him—knew a good story when he had one, and he had a very good one otherwise there would have been no call for the meeting that was taking place to take place. There was F.K. Pulp and four FBI men sitting in a semi-circle around his very large desk. In true Texas style, courteous style that is, he offered them breakfast and the only one to accept his gracious offer was FK Pulp, who he referred to as F.K. The four FBI men were so much alike in dress, build and looks that Ramblin' designated them by numbers, starting with number one on his right.

It was number three who explained the seriousness of the situation, telling him that National Security was involved, and that F.K.'s source or sources of information must forthwith be revealed.

Ramblin' said, "Sir, I don't know what you're talking about. The War Department and the United States Army has publicly denied the validity of the story; therefore, according to the logic of their stance, the story is invalid and by extension, the information on the source of the story is invalid; thereby making the source of the story, if not invalid, than certainly untrustworthy." Having said all of that he poured another shot of Wild Turkey and drank it.

Number four said, "Spreading false rumors—"

"I didn't know the story was a rumor," Ramblin' said, looking at F.K.

F.K. shrugged. "You never know when a rumor pops up and somehow becomes more than a rumor."

"Just suppose," Ramblin' said, "that something fluky is going on with every fourth round of fifty-caliber ammo, wouldn't you want to know about it in the interests of National Security?"

"I'll answer that one," said number four, distinguished from the other three by a small brown mole under his left eye and the fact that his eyes were black, while his three comrade's eyes were blue. "I wouldn't believe it unless it came from official sources. Those are the only sources I would trust."

F.K. whooped with laughter and so did Ramblin'.

The four Government men were totally disconcerted, and looked at each other with the hope of finding something that would give each of them aid and comfort and found nothing.

Finally number three said, "Mister Pulp we had a complete dossier on you."

"I would be surprised if you didn't, since I served with Wild Bill Donavan in the OSS, during the war, the war being World War II, gentlemen, and worked behind the lines, deep in France and later in Germany.

And I happen to know that little J Edger and Wild Bill, though on the same side, hated each other's guts . . . So you have my dossier, big fuckin ' deal. Give me a couple of days and I'll have all of your dossiers too."

"Impossible," number one said.

F.K. gave him a big Cheshire cat grin and said, "I got fifty bucks that says I will. What have you got?"

"None of us doubt that you still have very important contacts in DC," Number three said. "But we're not here to discuss those contacts."

"Why are you here?" Ramblin' asked. "It appears to me that there's a "tempest in a tea pot" when the government says there isn't even a tea pot."

Annoyed, number two said, "There is a source to the story and, like it or not, we will eventually find it."

F.K. threw up his hands, "Either arrest me or not, because you're sure as shit not getting one more word out of me. Ramblin', I got better things to do than sit here an' play word games with these guys." He stood. "I'll be back later today." And without looking at the four FBI men, he left the office.

"Tough man," Ramblin' commented after the door was closed.

* * *

F.K. didn't know whether he should be angry or amused. Since his time with Wild Bill, he didn't care much for Hoover's guys; they were strong arm men, in his opinion, wearing black suits not much different from the Mafia.

He went over to Short's desk, who gave him his usual bull dog look and asked, "What's the story?"

"Ramblin' is fly fishing them," F.K. answered.

"He's sure enough good at that."

"One of the best."

"I'm going out for a walk, be back in a little bit," F.K. said, clapping his ten gallon hat on his head.

Short didn't respond, and F.K. walked down the two flights of steps to the lobby, nodded to the Chicano who was sweeping the floor, and stepped out of the air-conditioned environment into a blistering hot morning. By afternoon, the temperature would hit a hundred and twenty degrees, and it was already mid-September.

He walked toward Alligator Park because that was the closest place where there were a few scraggily trees with green leaves on them. Blowing a few smoke rings as he walked, he thought about the situation that he had reported on; and the more he thought about it, two very distinct possibilities occurred to him: an overactive imagination had produced the story about every fourth round being a combination of tracer and nuclear. Exactly why this overactive imagination had been set in motion was a question that still had to be answered. But the second possibility, the one that burned so many asses in Bliss and Washington, meant that the story born out of an over active imagination cut close to the bone of truth, though not necessarily with 50-caliber tracers, probably with bigger stuff, like artillery shells.

By the time he reached Alligator Park, he was sweating profusely and needed the comfort of an air conditioned place to cool down and dry out. The El Paso Del Norte was not that far away, but it was further away than he was willing to walk and the Alligator Park Hotel was right in front of him, shabby though it was. He immediately opted for it; and as he walked across the park, he saw him and stopped. There he was sitting next to a driver in a Jeep. John Gault MacKenna, the man who, like Riley, Ace of Spies, was one of Wild Bill's best operatives, the man who saved his life.

F.K. shouted, he even started to run toward the Jeep, but the vehicle pulled away, leaving him breathless and even more perspired than he was before. F.K. hurried into the hotel and plopped down on a club chair whose springs were in sore need of repair.

F.K. summoned one of the baggage handlers, and handing him a five dollar bill told him to immediately bring two very large glasses of ice tea. With that done, he removed his hat, wiped his brow and said to himself, "Well, I'll be a son-of-a-bitch, if that wasn't JG MacKenna in that fucking jeep." The words were no sooner out of him, when he remembered the 2 on the jeep's bumper, but the other numbers that designated the jeep's unit were blurred, and there were many units whose numerical IDs began with the numeral 2.

The two glasses of ice tea that F.K. ordered were brought to him and placed on a small, portable table set up next to the club chair. He sipped the ice cold tea through a straw and found it sweetly refreshing.

F.K. was sufficiently well known to cause the manager, Mister Higgensbottom, to come out of his office to ask if "everything is satisfactory."

F.K. nodded and said that everything was satisfactory.

That would have ended their conversation, but Mister Higgenbottom, having little to do in office, took the opportunity to engage F.K. in a brief conversation about the Trees family, whose youngest son had experienced some rough treatment at the hands of the Mexican Police and *Federales* until he could properly identify himself. Higgensbottom was distantly related to the Trees on his mother's side. A scarecrow of a man, it was rumored he was worth a few million dollars and had in his salad days fathered no less than eighteen children with ten different Mexican women, all of whom worked in the hotel in various capacities.

F.K. hadn't paid any attention to the article; it was almost a side bar and not a very large one at that. The photo of Philip Trees took up more space than the copy.

"It's a cryin' shame that decent people are so poorly treated by those barbarians across the border," Higgensbottom lamented.

Knowing something about Philip's playfulness when it came to women or when he had half a load on, F.K. said, "I hear it takes a couple of guys to tango, or is it tangle?"

Higgensbottom wasn't sure what to make of that, and rather than find himself out on a limb in defense of a tree with which he had no contact, he said officiously, "I must get back to my work. It's been a pleasure speaking with you F.K."

They shook hands and F.K. began to suck up the second tea.

* * *

Carmine looked at his watch; the time registered was ten minutes to twelve. Something was very wrong. Polly was still at his desk and not first on the chow line. That fact was enough to make him think that something more than he already thought was going on; and if it was going on, he was sure that it had something to do with the story in the morning newspaper about the nuclear 50 caliber tracers.

Ordinarily Carmine wouldn't have given any thought to the story, but after Polly had read it aloud, he reread it and he began to see, or rather feel that there were certain connections between the newspaper story and MacKenna taking over the Heavy Weapons Section. And though the connections were very loose, they were tight enough for Carmine to come up with the conclusion that MacKenna was not only a plant, but he was there to implement the change from non-nuclear to nuclear-tracers. And if that was so, it was also the reason why Celenza wanted Trappaso as far away from the action as possible. After all, they were family and Celenza was protecting his own.

All of that thinking exhausted Carmine, and he was ready for a nap, but he was also hungry and the nap could wait until after he ate.

"You goin' to chow?" Carmine asked.

"Not hungry," Polly answered.

"You sick or somethin'?"

"Just not hungry."

MACKENNA'S PIECE

Carmine shrugged and left the Orderly Room.

* * *

Polly felt the great weight of loneliness on him; there was no one he could turn to for succor. Gibbs would sympathize with him, but do nothing to help him. His "friends" would help only if they got something in return, like no interest on their debts. He couldn't go to the police because the Trees owned them body and soul. Celenza was out of the picture because Polly thought that he was like "a fart in a wind storm." Besides, the Lieutenant was eyeball deep in Mackenna's transfer, and the shit from that was yet to hit the proverbial fan.

He paced the length of the Orderly Room that was exactly five strides wide, about fifteen feet. But pacing didn't solve it. If it did anything, it made him more aware of his predicament.

Suddenly, he stopped pacing and in a very audible voice said, "MacKenna." The sound of the man's name made Polly smile. This was the opportunity he'd been waiting for ever since MacKenna came into the unit and loaned money to several of the men without interest. In exchange for MacKenna's help, he'd offer him a share in the business. MacKenna would know exactly how to handle Philip Trees.

Happier than he'd been all morning, Polly left the Orderly Room and joined the Chow Line; it was a very long line.

57

* * *

F.K. Pulp returned to Ramblin's office, who scribbled a note that he was on the phone with J. Edgar Hoover. F.K. nodded, settled in the chair in front of Ramblin's desk, pushed back his hat and listened to one half of the conversation.

Ramblin' said, "You come down here with God's angels, an' you still won't get the source of the story."

Pause.

"Take that as gospel."

A long pause.

"Mister Hoover, do I sound like a Communist to you?"

Another long pause.

"Well, now that's a horse of different color, especially if that horse happens to be red."

Short pause.

"I'm not is the mood to play twenty questions."

Pause.

"Subpoena me if that makes you happy, and I'll do the same."

Pause.

"Yes, I will.

Pause.

"Thank you; it's been a lovely conversation," Ramblin' said; and putting the phone down, laughed heartily.

"You didn't show the man proper respect," F.K.said.

"Yea got that, didn't you?"

"Sure as shootin', and I'm damn proud of you," F.K. said.

"Well, another day another dollar," Ramblin' said. "But what I'd like to know is why those guys in Washington are so jumpy? To put it another way, what the hell did you stumble on that's put a hot poker up their collective asses from Bliss to Washington?"

F.K. took out a cigar from inside breast pocket, bit off the end and deposited it in the ash tray on the desk, lit it and blew two perfect smoke rings before he said, "Security is going to be drum tight, so my contacts at Bliss won't be worth a damn."

Ramblin' nodded.

"I'll think of something," F.K. said with not much optimism in the tone of his voice.

"Yeah, you usually do," Ramblin' answered.

"What about the jomokes who were here earlier?" F.K. asked.

Ramblin' waved his right hand to show it was 'kid's stuff.'

"That's why I got the call from the big man."

"How much trouble are we in, and how much trouble can we get into?"

Ramblin' shrugged.

"Maybe we'll get to meet Joe McCarthy?"

F.K. blew three more rings. "Think it might go that far?"

Ramblin' shrugged.

"Well, well, well, I guess I really will have to think of something," he said getting to his feet. "I'll let you know what tumbles my way, Ramblin ' "

"I'm sure you will."

F.K. left the office and headed for Frank's Trattoria; he was in the mood for Veal Parmesan, Mexican Style.

* * *

The distance between the newspaper's offices and Frank's was five blocks: two were short and three were long. Because of the heat, F.K. walked slowly. He was, of course thinking about the conversation he just had with Ramblin'. He admired the man for upholding the First Amendment of the Constitution that guarantees "the freedom of the press." That he might be summoned to Washington by the UHAC bunch didn't faze him. Once, while working for Wild Bill Donavan, he'd been picked up by the SS and questioned for twenty-two hours without interruption, during which he played the part of a simpleton and got away with it. Otherwise, he'd have been shot.

The recollection of that incident made him think of MacKenna, who he was sure he saw earlier in the jeep that belonged to a unit whose number began with 2. And that made him wonder how many unit numbers in Bliss began with 2? Not too many, he thought. If there were a half dozen, that would surprise him.

At that particular moment, he was directly across the street from the El Paso Del Norte Hotel where there were private phone booths, a fact that made him smile and brought out the dimples in cheeks. He crossed the street, entered the air-conditioned lobby and went to a phone booth, deposited a dime and dialed a number.

"Warrant Office Jekens here," the voice on the other end answered.

"Hey, Norbit, this is F.K. Got a question for you," F.K. said.

"No can answer," Norbit said.

"Yeah, I know security is tight assed," F.K. responded.

"You better believe it."

"You lookin' at your TOE?"

"Maybe."

"Good."

"How many units begin with the number two?"

"One."

"Any numbers after the two?"

"Four and Five."

"You're a sweetheart."

"Cut the shit, you owe me a dinner."

"I sure do," F.K. said.

"Infantry," Norbit said.

"In Bliss?"

"That's where the Army put them, and that's where they are."

"Good conversation," F.K. said.

"When do I collect my dinner?"

"Wednesday night, meet me in Manelos in Jaurez," F.K. said. "I'll treat you to more than a steak dinner."

"Wilco, over and out," Norbit said.

F.K. put the phone back on the cradle and for several moments didn't move. If it was MacKenna, and he was sure it was, what the hell was he doing in the two hundred and forty fifth Infantry Battalion? To find out, he phoned the 245th's Headquarters Company and spoke to Master Sargent Gibbs telling him he was MacKenna's cousin though he didn't give his name; and said it was urgent that MacKenna contact him. "Family problems," he told Gibbs. "Tell him I'll be in the El Paso bar at six this evening." *Cousin* was a code word used by the OSS to identify another operative.

Gibbs assured FK that MacKenna would be given the message.

F.K. ended the conversation with a dramatic "thank you," clicked off and immediately phoned Ramblin'. "It's the new infantry unit in Bliss," F.K. said without any preliminary conversation.

"Bliss is all Arty," Ramblin' answered.

"Was, now isn't."

"I'll have to chew on that for a while and maybe make a few calls."

F.K. laughed and clicked off. He was ready for lunch. By God, he suddenly realized he was hungry.

* * *

General Gunner was in "high dudgeon" as though he had forgotten that by the following Wednesday he would be relieved of his command and General Lewis Cannon, nickname Loose Cannon, would take over the command of Bliss, while he would be on his way to Washington with a new assignment not yet named. But that was still days away, even light years away as far as Gunner was concerned. What he wanted now was results; he wanted the son-of-a-bitch who leaked the story about the 50 caliber tracers with nuclear tips.

It was General Shot who reminded him that 50 Caliber tracers with nuclear tips did not exist. But specially fabricated artillery shells with a nuclear component were being experimented with in the Orange zone, a secret area deep inside the vast area of Bliss.

"So far," Shot continued, "the 245th is the only unit that uses 50 Calibers in their heavy weapons section."

Gunner, who was now drumming the fingers of his right hand on top of his desk, was still very angry, but he heard Shot and said, "Put a CID man in there and—"

"One is already there, Colonel John Gault MacKenna," Shot said.

"Why?"

"A shylocking operation."

"Contact him. This takes precedence," Gunner said. "What's his operational rank?"

"Soon to be a Sergeant First Class, Section Chief of the Heavy Weapons Section."

"An ideal position for this operation, code named Leaky Sieve."

"I have already alerted him," Shot said. "He was here earlier this morning."

"Wasn't he with Wild Bill's OSS?"

"Yes, sir."

Gunner made a humming-like sound that could have meant he was satisfied or dissatisfied; which one it would be depended completely on the throw of the mental dice that rattled around inside of his brain. This time they came up snake-eyes, and he said, still full of anger, "I'll show those sons-of bitches just who commands this fuckin' base. There will be a General Inspection on Saturday morning for the entire base, and that means I want every man out there, all eighty-two thousand."

Shot had no choice but to say, "Yes, Sir."

* * *

MacKenna's driver was Mastrangelo, called by his surname because his given name was Vincent, therefore Vinny. To avoid confusion between the two Vinnys in the company, Mastrangelo and Trappaso were their names of choice.

Mastrangelo was a young man of nineteen years who was also related to Celenza by marriage. His sister married George Mastrangelo and that made Vinny Mastrangelo his nephew. Young Mastrangelo was assigned to the Motor Pool, and under Captain Verhary's command. That morning Major Davidson, the XO, requested a jeep and driver to drive MacKenna to base headquarters.

Mastrangelo, who rarely thought of anything more than pussy, or the job that awaited him with Leo when he got out, did what he usually did when he was given an assignment. He shrugged his shoulders, took the trip ticket from the dispatcher, Arty Iscole, and drove off.

To him MacKenna was just another Sergeant on some sort of an errand at base Headquarters until Mastrangelo realized that MacKenna was not just another Sergeant.

MacKenna told him to park in the parking area for visitors, and then said, "I'll be a while. Why don't you go over to the canteen and wait for me there. I'll pick you up when I'm finished."

Mastrangelo agreed. Being inside an air conditioned space was a hell of a lot better than sitting in the hot sun.

A little more than an hour passed, and Mastrangelo was at a table enjoying a chocolate malted when he happened to look out of the window across from where he sat and there was MacKenna with a bird colonel and a one star general. The three of them yakked for a few minutes; then MacKenna shook hands with the bird colonel and the one star general, and walked away. A few moments later he entered the Canteen.

Mastrangelo didn't believe what he had just witnessed. Though new to the army, he had already learned that rank, like money in civilian life, made a difference. The more rank you had the more of everything you got. He knew that a Sergeant, even a Sergeant First Class doesn't yak with a bird colonel and a one star general, and doesn't shake hands with them. Even as he thought about what he had seen, he found himself looking up at MacKenna. Neither he nor MacKenna spoke during the ride back to Logan Heights. Whenever he glanced at the Sargent, he seemed to be somewhere else, at least in his head. The guy gave Mastrangelo the strange feeling that he had seen something he shouldn't have seen; and that made him feel very uncomfortable, a feeling he wasn't familiar with. And because he didn't know how to deal with it, he decided to speak to his best friend, Salvatore (Sal) O'Marie about it. Sal was one of three Medics who worked with Doctor Fragola.

But by the time Mastrangelo hit the noon chow line, he'd forgotten about it; and he and Sal had other things to speak about. Word was out that there would be a big Poker game Friday night and both of them were players.

* * *

As soon as F.K. Pulp entered Frank's Trattoria, he was snookered by the *maître d'*, Peppe Cervantes, who told him the two ladies in the booth in front of the one he usually occupies asked the bartender about him.

"Good looking?" F.K. asked.

Cervantes kissed his fingertips.

F.K. smiled, nodded and handed him two dollars.

"Good luck," Cervantes said.

"Fortune favors the bold," F.K. answered, and he boldly marched off.

In a matter of minutes, he was seated next to Silvia determined to find out whether or not she was a real blond, and at the same time also determined to discover if Angie's demure appearance was camouflage for a "hot number."

F.K. quickly confirmed what he already suspected: the husbands of the two women were in the 245th Infantry Battalion. Silvia's husband was a First Lieutenant and Angie's husband, a Sergeant. Silvia also mentioned the fact that the unit originally came from Brooklyn and was part of the New York National Guard before it was federalized.

Even as they spoke, F.K. critically examined the physical attractiveness of each of the women and decided that they were sufficiently endowed to warrant the risk, so he said, "Ladies, as a gentleman should, I will put all my cards of the table. I am married and have two children. My family lives in Las Cruses, New Mexico, which is a couple of hours drive from here. I see them on weekends. During the week, I lead a bachelor's life. I have an apartment near the university. If you ladies would care to spend a couple of hours with me in a more intimate atmosphere and in a more intimate way, I would be delighted to have you as my guests and introduce you to the pleasures of *ménage à trois*." Having said everything that needed to be said, F.K. waited for a response.

Both women tittered, somewhat nervously, and both blushed.

"Would you prefer to discuss it without me here?" F.K. asked because he needed to phone Short with a follow up on his previous story.

"What's a *ménage à trois*?' "Angie asked.

F.K. smiled. "Three people have sex, could be two women, like you and Silvia with me, or two men with one woman."

"Oh," she responded, blushing more intensely.

"If you'll excuse me, I'll be back in a few minutes," F.K. said left the booth.

* * *

"Short, put your best steno-girl on the phone," F.K. said. "I got a follow up story."

"Where are you?"

"Short, you ain't my mother," F.K. answered. "Put the gal on."

"Yeah, okay. Who's goin' to do the rewrite?"

"Me. I'll be by later. Now get the damn steno on."

Moments later a woman said, "I'm ready F.K."

"The United States Army has placed a special unit, the Two Hundred and Forty-Fifth Infantry Battalion from Brooklyn, New York, in Fort Bliss to test its Fifty Caliber nuclear ammunition. This unit, recently Federalized, is the first of several that will be testing the new ammunition. This information comes from unimpeachable sources.

"Fort Bliss was chosen for the site of the testing because of its size, and that parts of it are designated as top secret areas; and they require special clearance to enter.

"The question that arises from this experiment is its effect on the population of El Paso and nearby Juarez. Any ammunition that is destined for Fort Bliss must be shipped either by rail, truck or flown into nearby Biggs Air Force Base. Is it possible for a round or possibly more than one round to be defective and initiate a nuclear disaster?

"Got all of that?"

"Yes."

"Read it back to me."

"Good. Now put Short on."

"So?" Short asked.

"You heard it?"

"Yeah, you're going to put a blow torch to a few asses," Short said.

"I guess I will," F.K. laughed.

"When are you comin' in?"

"I'll be there by six."

"It's two now."

"I have some business to take care of," F.K. said and clicked off. For several moments, he didn't move and took stock of his situation. He knew the story would have consequences both good and bad. It would certainly boost his professional standing, and it would also irk the hell out of the Army and the FBI. Neither prospect bothered him. If they wanted to joust with him, he'd be more than willing to enter the lists. And with that, he left the phone booth. That was when he saw him, a man in a black suit, sitting at the bar, not too far away from the booth where Silvia and Angie were waiting for him.

F.K. returned to the phone booth, deposited a nickel and dialed the restaurant's phone number.

Cervantes answered.

"Peppe, this is F.K., there's a man at the bar close to where the two ladies are."

"I see him."

"Good."

"I want you to roust him, and not gently. He probably has a tape and a mini camera on him. I want them. Yeah, I owe you big time."

Cervantes laughed. "That's what I like about you F.K.; you sometimes bend the edges but never the middle."

"Once he's out of the way, tell the ladies that I'm terribly sorry but I wasn't able to keep my appointment with them, but something came up that demanded my immediate attention. Put their lunches on my tab and give them a couple of drinks on my tab."

"Anything else?"

"No," F.K. answered, and for a second time left the phone booth. He went behind a trellis interwoven with ivy so he was able to see exactly what was happening at the bar without being seen.

Two men entered the restaurant, went straight to the bar and said something to the man in the black suit, who protested. Suddenly, his jaw went slack.

F.K. didn't see the gun, but he was sure the man at the bar felt the push of a gun muzzle against his side. He was frisked by one of the two men, and relieved of a snub-nose .38, a tape and a Minox camera before he was escorted outside. The action took less than two minutes, and was carried without disturbing any of the diners.

When F.K. saw Peppe go to the booth where Silvia and Angie were, he left the restaurant feeling good about himself. He had avoided leading the two ladies "down the primrose road of dalliance" and possible trouble for himself later.

CHAPTER V

At the Officer's Club, General Gunner was finishing his second Martini at lunch, and was considerably mellower than he was earlier when he ordered a General Inspection for Saturday. Taking advantage of Gunner's mellowness, General Shot said, "Sir, don't you think a General Inspection on Saturday would be too close to the general review planned for General Lewis Cannon on the following Wednesday?

Gunner continued to stare at his luncheon plate of corn beef and cabbage. He was more of a lunch nibbler than an eater, and more of a drinker than a nibbler.

Shot repeated the question; but this time he also added, "General Cannon will arrive at thirteen hundred tomorrow, and might be confused by the two parades, and think that both were for him, to honor—"

Gunner's head bobbed up. "Damn, why didn't I think of that?" he questioned. And before Shot could answer, he said, "Cancel the fucking order. We don't need two fucking parades. Besides, Cannon, in my opinion, isn't fit to command a damn troop of cats, let alone a base this big."

Shot neither agreed nor disagreed. But he was pleased that he had not relayed the order for the Saturday parade when Gunner gave it. Working with Gunner for the past two years gave him some insight into the general's behavior. He was a man of quick decisions and frequently made the wrong ones.

"I'm damn glad I caught that one," Gunner said.

"Yes, sir," Shot answered.

* * *

MacKenna stared moodily out of the jeep as Mastrangelo turned into the Company Area on Logan Heights. MacKenna intuited that the story in the newspaper was in some way connected to him taking over the Heavy Weapons Section of A Company, but exactly how he couldn't even begin to guess.

"Headquarters," Mastrangelo announced.

MacKenna, roused out of his thoughts, said, "Thanks for the ride." He left the jeep and went into Headquarters to drop off a couple of envelopes for ExO Major Davidson, at the Message Center. He was about to leave and head back to the Company Area with the hope that he'd still be able to get some chow even though it was twelve-forty-five when Gibbs spotted him and called him to his desk.

"You were supposed to report here this morning," Gibbs said.

"I wouldn't know about that," MacKenna answered.

"The orders—"

"Sergeant, the order given to me by Corporal Polly gave me the temporary rank of acting Sergeant First Class, Section Chief of the Heavy Weapons Section of Company A."

"Impossible!"

"I happen to have a copy of the order in my pocket. Yours and the Colonel's signatures are on it."

Gibbs trembled with anger.

"I must get to the mess hall or I'll miss lunch," MacKenna said.

"You can be sure I'll get to the bottom of this," Gibbs growled. "And by the way your cousin called. Said he'd be in touch with you."

"Thanks," MacKenna said and left Battalion Headquarters. As he walked slowly up the hill to A Company's area, he wondered who his cousin was.

* * *

Silvia and Angie were disappointed. They had decided to give *ménage à trois* a try on the basis that it would only be a one shot deal, and since both of them realized how uneducated they were when it came to sex, they saw F.K.'s offer as a way to further their knowledge. But since that wasn't going to happen, neither one was willing to completely dismiss the idea from their imaginations. And it was Silvia who suggested that it might be fun to figure out the various combinations that might have taken place between F.K. and the two of them.

"We'll do it with stick figures," Silvia said. "I'll draw them on a napkin."

Angie agreed.

"Each one of us will watch while the other two do it," Silvia said, busy creating the necessary stick figures.

"Does that mean F.K. would have watched us?" Angie whispered. "I mean would we do..." She couldn't finish saying what she started to say.

Silvia stopped drawing and looked at her. "I don't know. I guess."

Then, she too stopped speaking.

"I've never done…" Angie began.

"Me neither," Silvia responded.

"Maybe doin' this—I mean figurin' out the combos ain't a good idea," Angie said.

"Maybe not," Silvia answered capping her pen and crumpling the napkin.

* * *

At just about quitting time, sixteen-thirty, 1st Lieutenant Patrick Shanahan, also known as Lard Ass by the men, stood in front of Warrant Officer Gene Semelinski's desk and said, "I want Private MacKenna's two-oh-one file."

Bleary-eyed, Semelinski looked up from the pile of papers in front of him. Shanahan's voice barely penetrated the roaring in his head that was like a freight train of noise left over from the previous night's hangover.

Shanahan was Battalion's S-2 (Intelligence) Officer, and sometime during the day he picked up on the fact that Gibbs was arranging a transfer of a new man into his section, a draftee with a couple of PhDs after his name and that immediately made him suspicious. Shanahan was constantly on the lookout for "Commies and fellow travelers." The story in the morning's newspaper and the Colonel's meeting were like breaths blown on kindling to start the fire going. His job, as he saw it, was to keep the Battalion a hundred percent American. Already there were too many foreign types in it. He was particularly wary of smart ass college graduates, especially those that came from New York City colleges or Ivy League Universities.

Semelinski squinted up at Shanahan and said, "Major Davidson has it."

Shanahan flushed. The major was his chief nemesis. All of the officers knew the Major considered him slightly above an idiot, and that, according to the Major, would be stretching his evaluation of Shanahan's intelligence.

"Did he say why he wanted it?" Shanahan asked.

"He didn't have to," Semelinsky answered. "Remember he's the Battalion's XO."

Shanahan was stymied.

"Anything else Lieutenant?" Semelinsky asked. "It's past closing time."

"Closing time?"

"You know, sixteen hundred and we're done for the day."

Shanahan's face reddened again. He was angry, frustrated in his attempt to get hold of MacKenna's 201 file, and by Semelinsky's remark about it being "quitting time." His eyes narrowed down and he said, "The Army is twenty four hours a day, seven days a week. And that goes for Warrant Officers as well as everyone else." He was shouting by the time he finished speaking.

A moment before, Major Davidson opened the door of his office and heard Shanahan ride Semelinsky. "What's the problem?" he asked walking toward the two of them.

As soon as they heard Davidson's voice, they responded. Shanahan faced him and came to attention, while Semelinsky remain seated and said, "Sir, I've just been informed that we're on a twenty-four hour, seven days a week schedule."

Davidson, a short wiry built man, looked up at Shanahan's fat red face, and said, "We are indeed on a twenty-four hour, seven days a week schedule."

Shanahan almost breathed a sigh of relief, but then the Major added, "But to fit the reality in which we find ourselves, quitting time is sixteen hundred hours unless the man chooses to work beyond that hour or has been assigned extra-duty."

Shanahan's kaki shirt became stained with dark blotches of sweat. He almost shook his head. Semelinsky, a bohunk and Davidson, a Jew, were on his list of foreigners that he wanted to get rid of.

Davidson, now squinting at Shanahan, asked, "When and who changed my operating orders?"

"Sir, I was only speaking symbolically."

The Major's gray eye's sparkled mischievously. "How does one speak symbolically? I thought only poets and novelists do that."

"Sir, Christ spoke symbolically."

"Are you comparing what you said with the words of Jesus Christ?"

Shanahan, who was a practicing Catholic, was flummoxed by the Major's question. No matter how he answered it, Davidson wouldn't miss the opportunity to further rag him.

The Major laughed, and said, "You're a little bit like one of those Wooly Mammoths that got themselves caught in the La Brier tar pits, aren't you Lieutenant?

"I suppose so," Shanahan answered meekly.

"Suppose," Davison said. "I know no: 'suppose.' It leaves too much wiggle room. Either you are or you're not."

To be out of his misery, Shanahan was willing to admit to anything short of murder and pederasty.

Semelinsky, whose head had been the right of way for scores of rattling freight trains, found he was devoid of that noise and enjoying what was taking place in front of his desk. He managed to keep a straight face though he really wanted to laugh.

Shanahan's shirt was now soaking wet; and he felt the droplets of moisture run down his legs and in his crotch. "Sir," he began, "I originally came here to examine Private MacKenna's two-oh-one file. And—"

"Too many people are interested in Private MacKenna," Davidson said. "So, I put a Q-Clearance on it."

"But that's only for personnel who handle nuclear weapons," Shanahan protested.

"Who knows what the future will bring," Davidson said with a broad smile.

"Sir, I only wanted to authenticate—"

"Do you have Q-Clearance?"

"No, sir."

"Permission denied," Davidson snapped; then, as an afterthought he added, "Dismissed."

* * *

Shanahan was so unnerved by his encounter with Davidson that he went to Juarez and paid a prostitute five dollars in Manelo's to regain it, though the next morning he would go to confession to purify his "sin sick soul." But it didn't happen with the woman; he couldn't get it up no matter how she ministered to his very limp cock. It was not only thought about Davidson who stood in the way of his erection; it was also the whole damn business of Q clearance. He didn't know too much about it, other than it was required by those individuals who are involved in some way with nuclear experiments or handle nuclear material.

He reasoned from what Davidson said that the unit was about to go nuclear with its 50 caliber machine guns or it was going to be converted to a nuclear artillery unit, and the lynchpin was Private MacKenna. Arriving at this conclusion after having three straight shots of Glenlivit, he left Manelo's convinced that something "big was in the offing."

* * *

F.K. was back at Shot's desk promptly at six as he said he would be, and Shot said, "Ramblin' wants to see ya."

"Thought he might want to," F.K. said.

Shot smiled, something he seldom did. "This is sure the biggest one you'll ever catch."

F.K. winked and headed for Ramblin's office. He knocked twice before opening the door.

"Can't you wait for me to say, 'Come in?'"

F.K. dropped into the chair in front of Ramblin's desk. "Waste of time," he said.

"What if I had my head between some woman's thighs?"

"I'd wait until you were finished, and maybe ask if I could have a go at it too."

Ramblin' guffawed. "Yeah, you would... Now tell me have we got the bull by its balls or are we just blowin' smoke."

"A little of both," F.K. said, and he explained, that the information came from the wives of two of the unit's men. But from the way everyone in the government is jumping around, my guess is that I'm damn close to something that I shouldn't be."

Ramblin' cut the tip of two cigars and handed one cigar to F.K. After they blew a couple of smoke rings, Ramblin' said, "Plan on being called by HUAC."

F.K. nodded. "I plan on packin' tonight."

Ramblin' opened the top draw of his desk and took out a stack of hundred dollar bills. He counted out twenty of them and pushed them across the desk. "That's for openers. There's more if needed."

"Thanks," F.K. said as he put the bills in his wallet.

"I figure the subpoenas should come by Monday," Ramblin' said.

"That's about right," F.K. answered.

"Okay, now go an' gussie up your story," Ramblin' said.

F.K.'s follow up story went over the wire at 9 P.M. By 9:15 the phones in the office began to ring; but no one was there to pick them up and speak to the individual who called.

* * *

That same afternoon MacKenna attended a briefing by Sergeant Joseph Katz, the Battalion's Operation Sergeant, who, according to what MacKenna heard from some of the other non-coms attending the meeting, was the brains of the Ops section, while Major Connelly, the officer in charge of the section, spent most of his day reading about fly-fishing, the sport to which he was addicted.

A scale model of the area in which the maneuvers would take place was set up in Battalion Headquarters. All of the Battalion Officers were present, including the Colonel. Using a pointer, Katz explained that the invading force would be coming out of Mexico, "and it was our mission to stop them from capturing this cross roads and this rail head." And he used the pointer to indicate where each one was. "Headquarters Company will be located here in this gully, between the crossroads and the railhead," he explained. "The Battalion's four companies will protect the gully it, the rail head, and the cross roads by placing themselves in front of Headquarters Company and the two enemy objectives, Able and Baker Companies to the east and Charlie and Dog Companies to the west. Detailed maps, additional instructions and passwords will be forthcoming. The maneuvers will last three days. Our ability to accomplish the assigned mission will be judged by Fourth Army officers. Any questions?"

MacKenna raised his hand.

"Please state your name and rank before you ask the question," Katz said.

"Acting Sergeant MacKenna."

"Ask your question."

"There's a ridge line about a quarter of a mile back of our positions according to the scale model in front of us," MacKenna noted.

Katz smiled and said, "I did a statistical analysis of the situation and found that our opposing forces will have a fifty to one chance of making it to that ridge line once they initiate a frontal assault, which they will do because they have no other option."

MacKenna wasn't going to argue the point. He would let Katz drown in his own mistakes.

The officers were pleased with the presentation, and the Colonel congratulated Major Connelly and his staff for their fine work.

MacKenna caught Major Davidson's eyes and shook his head. Davidson responded with a nod.

At the end of the meeting, MacKenna loitered in Battalion Headquarters, feeling certain that Katz would button hole him. He had heard about Katz almost from the day he arrived in the Battalion. He was the whiz kid from Brooklyn College with degree in mathematics. And of course, Katz had heard about MacKenna after the Saturday morning inspection when MacKenna suggested that something might be amiss with Celenza's right eye.

Katz did indeed seek MacKenna out, and wanted to know why he didn't ask to be assigned to the Ops section.

"I'm a field man," MacKenna answered.

"Any time you change your mind, let me know and Connelly will make it happen.

MacKenna thanked him and asked how accurate his statistical analysis was.

"Plus or minus ten percent."

MacKenna accepted the answer with a nod.

"What made you ask?"

"Just curious," MacKenna answered lightly.

"Are you going to be at the big game tonight?" Katz asked, who himself was an inveterate poker player and almost always a loser.

"Polly invited me," MacKenna said, "so I guess I'll go."

"See you there," Katz answered and joined Major Connelly, who was talking to the Colonel.

* * *

As soon as MacKenna stepped into bright sunlight, he saw his "cousin," Frank Kingston. He was standing outside of a white Caddy.

"Holy shit," F.K. exclaimed, "what the fuck are you doing here?"

MacKenna pointed to the Caddy and said, "Let's drive."

"Anything you say," F.K. answered.

Five minutes later, F.K. pulled over to the side of the road, cut the engine and rolled down the windows.

By that time MacKenna had made the connection between Frank Kingston and F.K. Pulp.

"How many years has it been?" F.K. asked.

"At least five."

"My God did we live a life?"

MacKenna nodded.

"What the fuck are you doing here?"

"CID," MacKenna said.

F.K. looked closely at his face. "Something is wrong, you haven't aged."

"Last mission for Wild Bill, got pretty well—no matter. Had plastic surgery."

"Bad mission?"

"Got betrayed and the Krauts—well, you know what they can do once they get started."

"What's your real rank?"

"Colonel."

"Planning on staying in?"

"Not too much longer if I make Brigadier," MacKenna answered. "I have hopes of doing some writing about the war and teaching at a college or university."

F.K. took that in without commenting on it. He could easily arrange a teaching position for him in the El Paso campus of the University of Texas. He and the President of the college, Joshua Payson, were golfing buddies.

"And you're getting the wrong people or riled up," MacKenna said.

F.K. grinned.

"Take it from me, there isn't any fifty-caliber nuclear tipped ammo."

F.K. threw up his hands. "I believe you, but from the reaction to my stories, I suspect that there must be some type of hot ammo here, probably in seventy-five mm or bigger."

"That was my guess too," MacKenna said. "But your pushing on the Two Forty Fifth Battalion will entangle—"

"By the by, what the hell are you doing there?"

"A two for five operation going on, but that's not for public consumption."

"Understood."

"Married?

"Twice; the second one seems to be working. I have two kids with Anna-Mari. What about you?"

"Killed in an auto crash."

"Tough."

"Any kids?"

"Didn't have time; we were only married a couple of months."

"Any prospects?"

MacKenna shook his head. Lots of wiggling, but nothing I'd want to settle down with."

"I expect to be called by the HUAC committee and that goes also for the publisher, Ramblin'."

"Watch your ass; those guys are killers in white shirts and flashy ties."

"I certainly will."

"I've got to get back to my section," MacKenna said.

"We'll have dinner soon," F.K. said, handing MacKenna his card. "Give me a call when you're free."

MacKenna took the card, put it in his wallet and said, "We go into the field in a week. I'll call you after that."

"If I'm not in Washington or in jail, we'll meet," F.K. said, starting the car, and then making a U-turn.

* * *

There were two games going on in the Mess Hall: Poker, where Polly was the dealer; and Black Jack, where Gibbs was the dealer. In addition to the Sergeants and officers from the 245th there were a few men from Brigade.

Both Polly and Gibbs wore the requisite green shades. Some of the players wore sunglasses to prevent other players from reading their eyes. Beer was available and cost twenty-five cents a glass. The concession was operated by one of Polly's friends. Anything stronger than beer could be had for a dollar a shot. That too was handled by another one of Polly's friends.

Everything that MacKenna saw was illegal. With one phone call, he could have ended the entire operation, but he also would have ensnared those men who only there to gamble and were not part of Gibbs' and Polly's organization. He only wanted Gibbs and Polly; without them there wouldn't be an organized gambling operation.

MacKenna chose to play poker, and purposefully lost a few rounds. At the table with him were there were the men from Brigade. One in particular stood out from the rest, a Master Sergeant, whose name was Jack Leeson, an ex-paratrooper with the Hundred and First Division. He'd been at Bastogne, and like every other National Guardsmen who were veterans of the Second World War, he was back on active duty when the Brigade was federalized.

Leeson was a broad shouldered man of middling height, with fair skin, blond hair and blue eyes. To MacKenna he looked more like a German than

Germans did. He was a loudmouth who made running comments on every hand that was played. He also had a lot on money on him because he continually raised the ante that started at a quarter a round and now was up to a dollar.

Suddenly Leeson announced, "That's it for me. I have a royal flush and the pot is mine." And then with a big grin, he added, "And so the South wins the War of Northern Aggression."

His buddies cheered him.

"How much do you think is in that pot?" MacKenna asked. He'd been counting cards and there was no way Leeson could have a royal flush unless he palmed a few.

"A couple of Cs," Polly said.

"Double or nothing," MacKenna quietly offered.

"You're joking?" Leeson asked.

In the same quiet tone, MacKenna said, "The South lost the Civil War."

Leeson's face reddened. "Are you accusin' me of lyin'?"

"No. But the fact is that the South lost the war."

Leeson looked at the pot and then at MacKenna; then back at the pot, said, "If I win the South won, if I—"

A couple of his buddies tried to tell him that the South had lost the war. But he answered, "Yeah, but it's gonna win this time."

"Polly, open a new deck," MacKenna said, "and give it to me."

"Sure," he answered.

MacKenna handed the new deck to Leeson, who riffled it and handed it back to MacKenna, who also riffled it; then, he cut it into three approximately equal parts, recombined them and handed the deck back to Polly. "You shuffle them and then deal."

By this this time, everyone in the room was gathered around the poker table. The Blackjack game had stopped, and Gibbs took up his position directly behind Polly.

"Five," Leeson said, after the first was dealt.

"I'll see that and raise it by five." MacKenna answered.

Leeson asked for a card.

MacKenna stood pat.

"I'll raise you ten," Leeson said.

"Ten it is," MacKenna answered.

The betting continued until there was two grand or more in the pot.

"I'm tapped out; I fold," Leeson said and spread a full house of Spades on the table.

MacKenna nodded and said, "A busted flush. Seems like the North won that bloody war."

"I'll remember you, Sergeant," Leeson said.

"You do that," MacKenna answered, "because next time, it will be in different circumstances.

"And what's that supposed to mean?"

MacKenna shrugged. "Anything you want it to mean," he said and gathered his winnings.

* * *

"You sure bluffed him," Polly said, not without admiration.

"Done it before," MacKenna answered. "A guy like him is—" He stopped himself from saying *is trouble*. But that might cue Polly to the fact that he wasn't who he appeared to be.

"I'd say there was about two Gs in the pot, and the House's take is ten percent."

"Fifteen percent on anything over five hundred," Polly said.

MacKenna counted out the requisite amount, and stuffed the rest of it in the pockets of his fatigues.

Gibbs stood by, but didn't say anything, except, "I expect to see you in Headquarters tomorrow morning."

MacKenna shrugged.

"I don't know what game you're playing; but I sure as hell will find out," Gibbs said.

Again MacKenna shrugged. He disliked officious men like Gibbs almost as much as he disliked guys like Leeson, who threw their weight around differently from the Gibbs of the world, but threw it nonetheless.

Gibbs picked up the House's cut, nodded to Polly, and ram rod straight, left the mess all.

"I'd say he was pissed," MacKenna commented.

"Wait till he sees the orders," Polly said.

"Time to call it a night," MacKenna announced. "We've got about twenty minutes before lights out."

Polly agreed.

"You better go," MacKenna told him.

"I thought we'd walk back to the Company area together," Polly said, thinking it was the opportunity he'd been waiting for.

"Leeson and a couple of his buddies are probably waiting for me outside," MacKenna said.

"You're not serious, are you?"

"Do you see me smiling or hear me laughing?"

"Even alone that son-of-a-bitch is a bruiser, and with a couple of his buddies—they'll tear you apart."

MacKenna didn't answer.

Polly dug into his fatigue pocket and pulled out the .32 caliber automatic he'd taken off of Philip Trees. "This might give us an edge."

"It also might land us in prison. Put it away, Polly."

"If they're out there, you don't stand a chance in hell against them," Polly said.

"Go. I'll take care of—"

Suddenly the door opened, and Leeson and two of his buddies stepped inside the mess hall. "Just hand over the pot and no one will get hurt," Leeson said.

"What you're doing is called robbery," MacKenna said. If it was Leeson and one of his buddies, he might have taken them on; but with a third guy there, he knew he didn't have a chance. And Polly wouldn't count for much in a brawl.

"I don't give a fuck what's it's called," Leeson answered moving closer to MacKenna and Polly.

"I'm going to give you—"

Leeson started to move.

MacKenna saw Carmine before Polly did. He'd forgotten Carmine pulled Sergeant of the Guard. Mastrangelo was with him. Both were armed, Carmine with a .45 and Mastrangelo with an M-1.

"Freeze. All of you down on the floor. Now," Carmine barked pushing the muzzle of the 45 into Lesson's back. "On the floor. Spread eagle. Polly frisk 'em."

"Brass knucks and a thirty-eight," Polly said, showing them to Carmine.

"You want the MPs here?" Carmine asked.

MacKenna shook his head. "We don't want to give the battalion or the Brigade a black eye," he said to Carmine and Mastrangelo. "We'll handle it ourselves." He turned to Leeson and his buddies. "Okay, on your feet. Your brass knuckles and thirty-eight are confiscated. And not a fucking word of complaint about that."

"I'm going to let you thugs off easy," MacKenna added. "None of you will be charged with anything; but if anyone of you open your mouth about what happened here tonight, you'll be on the first fucking flight to Korea. Understand? I want to hear it. Do you understand?"

The three said they understood what MacKenna said.

"Okay, now get the hell out of here. If either you show up in the battalion's area, unless it's on official business, your ass is grass and you'll be on your way to Korea before you can wipe your ass," MacKenna said. "Understood?"

"Understood," Leeson said. "But we still have a score to settle."

* * *

"You guys showed up at the right time," MacKenna said.

"Me and Mastrangelo were checkin' the guard out, and we saw those three guys outside the mess hall," Carmine explained. "Mastrangelo said he heard you won big, so I figured those hooples were up to no good."

"Thanks," MacKenna said. "The three of them would have hurt us real bad."

Carmine agreed. He also knew that any other officer would have called MPs and that clued him off into thinking that MacKenna had his own reason for not doing that. And that, in turn, made him think that MacKenna might not be who or what everyone else thinks he is. The idea that MacKenna was some sort of "plant" came back to him. But he couldn't begin to guess what sort of "plant" MacKenna might be.

"Let's call it a night," Polly said, switching off the mess hall's lights.

"Oh, by the way, we've been put on standby," Carmine said to MacKenna, who answered with a nod. It was a routine operational procedure that occurred at least once a week, sometimes for as long as seventy-two hours. The next alert, should it come, would be yellow; and that would cause a flurry of activity to make sure that if that status changed to red, the battalion would be ready to act in whatever capacity Brigade designated.

The men bid each other good night. Carmine and Mastrangelo went off to check on the rest of guards, while MacKenna and Polly headed toward their respective hutments.

MacKenna paused outside of his hutment and looked up. The sky was cloudless and the stars intensely brilliant. He located the North Star, smiled and entered the hutment.

* * *

Even after taking two sleeping pills, Celenza couldn't sleep, not after what Silvia told him about her conversation with Angie and then with F.K. Pulp that very afternoon. He couldn't really blame Silvia for blabbing; he had told her about something he'd read in some magazine or other. It was bullshit, nothing more. But it had become something more thanks to F.K. Pulp, who picked up the story while eavesdropping on a conversation between Silvia and Angie. That was bad enough. But that afternoon, they actually told Pulp the name of the unit, the 245th Infantry Battalion. The morning newspaper was sure to carry that story and possibly more.

He was so upset that, even though Silvia offered him the delights of oral sex again, he couldn't even manage an erection and turned his back to her.

* * *

Silvia couldn't sleep either. But the cause or causes of her insomnia were very different from her husband's. Earlier at supper table she'd had asked him if he knew what *ménage à trois* was, and he said, "It has something to do with eating—like *mange a tres*. Probably it was some fancy Italian dish."

"Yeah, it has something to do with eating," she answered and let the subject drop.

But in bed it came back to her, especially what she and Angie spoke about before they too dropped the subject. But she was alone with her own thoughts and she wondered what she and Angie might do while F.K. or someone like him watched. Her upbringing told her that those were impure thoughts, and that she was in danger of going to hell if she continued with them. Though she wore her religion lightly, it wasn't light enough to avoid thinking about the consequences of imagining what she and Angie might do given the "right circumstances."

They had seen each other naked many times in the locker room at pool on the main base, and each of them commented on the other's body. Angie was dark skinned while Silvia was light. Angie had a black pussy; Silvia hardly had any hair, the rest was blond. Angie's breasts were high, with large nipples; Silvia's breasts were like half-moons tipped with small nipples. Both had supple bodies, Angie's was more compact, and Silvia had longer legs.

Despite her fear that she would burn in hell for what she was thinking, she couldn't stop thinking about Angie in the way that she'd never before thought about her. And when she finally slept, her dreams were filled with stick figures and the various configurations that evolved out of what little she knew about the *ménage à trois*.

* * *

Carmine sat at Gibbs' desk. He was about to close his eyes and enjoy a brief snooze when the phone

93

rang. As he picked up the phone, he glanced at his watch: it was 01:30. "The Two Hundred and Forty Fifth, Infantry Battalion, Sergeant Carmine Valdez, here."

"This is Lieutenant Crumb, One Hundred and First Infantry Brigade; all Brigade Units go to Red Alert. Repeat Red Alert.

"Roger that," Carmine said, immediately notifying Captain Walters of the change of status.

Within minutes Colonel Miller, Major Davidson and all of the other staff and line officers were told to report back to the company. The guards went from hutment to hutment shouting, "Red Alert. Fall out. Red Alert."

All of the lights in the company area were turned on. Orders for the men to pack their gear came down from Headquarters. Rifles and ammo were issued. A three-day supply of food was issued to each man, canteens were filled. All of this was accomplished with a great deal of confusion.

Roll call was repeated several times. Several men were missing; officially their whereabouts were unknown, and they were marked as being AWOL, Absent without Leave.

The men were ordered to wear full combat gear and that included a steel helmet, web belt, complete with addition ammo-pouches, a bayonet and scabbard for it.

The rumor that quickly spread was that "this was it: they were going to be shipped to Korea." Phone calls at the pay phone booths were off-limits to all personnel.

Everyone was tense, but the grimmest looking men were those who had seen action during the WWII, and wondered if they'd be lucky enough to survive fighting in Korea as well.

At 02:30 the order came from Brigade to the Captain Verhey to send ten trucks to the southwest railhead. Verhey became so excited, he began to stutter and ten trucks became "te-te-tw-tw--nty twu-fucks--to the sow-vest-nail head." But the drivers were used to his stuttering and knew he meant the south-west railhead.

An armed guard rode shotgun in each truck. A manned 30 caliber machine-gun was mounted on top of each cab. Iscole, the dispatcher, gave each driver a map of the route he was to follow to the rail head and then back to the company area.

The men of the 245th and the Brigade waited for the order that would set them in motion, but nothing more came from Base headquarters.

The Army was famous for its "Hurry up and wait" attitude, and the men of the 245th waited impatiently for something to happen. They smoked and cursed, cursed and smoked.

At 03:45 the trucks with their blacked-out lights were sighted turning into the Company Motor Pool. And when they stopped, Verhey ran from his orderly room to the lead truck. "What the fuck—"

At that precise moment the four hundred men that had been dispersed on the twenty trucks at the rail head began to leap off the rear of each truck and were ordered by their officers and non-coms to form up in ten ranks of twenty men, each carrying a duffel bag.

A light colonel stepped forward, saluted Verhey, and said, "Lieutenant Colonel Samuel Smarts, commander of this contingent of men assigned to the Two Hundred and Forty Fifth Infantry Battalion, Logan Heights, and Fort Bliss, Texas."

Verhey returned his salute, introduced himself and said, "We ain't goin' to Korea?"

"Not yet," Smarts said.

Verhey took off his steel helmet and helmet liner, and scratching his head, he asked, "What the hell are we goin' to do with you guys?"

* * *

Earlier, when Celenza was ordered to report back to Battalion because its status had been changed to "red alert," tears were shed by him and Silvia. Each was afraid they might never see one another again. There were hugs and kisses, and words of endearment as well as instructions from Celenza as to what Silvia should do if he should not come back.

The same scene, or something similar to it, took place between Vinny and Angie, and all of the married couples, who were living off base. It was for all of them an awakening to the stark reality that their lives were about to change, that permanence of their holy vows had no meaning for the army, that their husbands and sweethearts belonged not to them but to the United States Army.

Alone with her two children and the sleep-in maid, Silvia sent everyone back to bed, poured a goodly amount of Chianti into a tall glass, and sat at the kitchen table and thought about her future and the future of her children—her children because they might be fatherless for years or the rest of their lives. Despite her parochial background at home and in school—she graduated from St. Elizabeth's High School for Girls in Brooklyn—she still possessed a degree of independence, or as the sisters called it, "a stubborn streak" that made it possible for her to think without any mystical camouflage of the reality of her situation. There were literally dozens of things that she would have to attend to, like packing, arranging to ship everything in the apartment back to Brooklyn, arranging transportation for her and the children . . . The list grew and became a very long one as she finished drinking wine which led her to pour an additional half glass because she wasn't ready to stop thinking about her future.

With Tom gone, it would be the first time in her life that she would be completely on her own, at least for the time that she would have to be in El Paso. Once back in Brooklyn she'd again be surrounded by family, especially if she moved back into her old apartment, a four room apartment in a two story building owned by Tom's parents, who occupied the apartment on the ground floor. Though they were nice people, she and the children would be under their "watchful eyes" forever, and if Tom didn't make it back and another man entered her life how would they react?

Though distraught, the wine was having its effect. Her thoughts seemed to be exploding like firecrackers or zooming through her brain like multi-colored rockets. And thinking about another man entering her life, exploded into "the rocket's red glare" of Angie's naked body and she and Angie on top of F.K. Pulp . . . "Enough," she said out loud, waving the salacious image away. "Enough." And she managed to walk into the bedroom and fall on to bed, where she quickly fell asleep.

CHAPTER VI

Morning wasn't greeted with cheers. The men were bushed. At the most they got two hours of sleep. The new contingent of men were divided into groups of forty and slept on the floors of the five mess halls, one for each company of the battalion.

Two roll calls were held; and afterwards, those men that cared to eat, and that was most of them, went to breakfast only to find that there wasn't enough food for all of them. SOS, which was kindly called, "shit on a shingle," but was in reality chipped beef in a concoction of cream sauce, was in great demand. Bacon and eggs were premium dishes and went to those men who were first on line. But many of the men were forced to settle for a couple of slices of bread and a cup of coffee.

Sergeant LA Santi, Headquarters' Company's chief cook made a special trip to the base quartermaster's at 03:00 to ask for more food. The Duty Officer said, "Your roster says you got eight hundred men in your battalion, not twelve hundred."

No matter how LaSanti argued the situation, the Duty Officer wasn't moved. "You got four hundred more men they're your problem, not mine. When I get a change in your roster that says you have twelve hundred men, I'll authorize more rations.'

There was nothing LaSanti could do to change the situation, except to report it to Carmine, who reported it to Celenza, who said, "That's just another fuckin' problem to add to my list of fuckin' problems."

Carmine and Polly took Celenza's answer to mean, "Don't fucking bother me with your shit." And they weren't far off the mark in their interpretation. Celenza was terrified that Silvia's conversations with F.K. would soon involve him; and because of that he saw himself accused of "God knows what" and standing Courts Martial for a crime he didn't commit.

Because there were eighty new men in the Company, Polly and Carmine were deluged with paper work, and neither of them had time to either reflect on or speak about their previous night's experience. But the bluff MacKenna pulled was the topic of the conversations of the men of the 245th, in addition to their griping about the "shitty" breakfast that they "had to make do with."

Even before the new men were bedded down in the mess halls, Lieutenant Colonel Samuel Smarts informed Lieutenant Colonel Miller that all of his men were RA, regular Army, and had completed their sixteen weeks of basic training.

This meeting took place in front of the entire Battalion and the contingent of newly arrived troops.

"And furthermore," Smarts added, "they have all their necessary shots."

Bleary-eyed Colonel Miller answered, "We'll find something for them to do while we—" He let go of the sentence before he finished it because his mind went blank. Not exactly blank, but damn close to it. He hadn't the slightest idea of what to do with the new arrivals.

"We'll have to work out some sort of command arrangement," Smarts said.

Miller grasped the significance of that remark; and he said, "I'm in command of the Two Hundred and Forty Fifth Battalion, and that applies to any men assigned to it, Colonel."

Smarts answered with a salute, which Miller returned.

But when morning came, Miller was morose. Smarts and his men posed a problem he didn't know how to solve, and was reluctant to ask Davidson for his advice, since he left most of the battalion's problems for him to solve. But this one, he thought, should be his because it directly involved him.

It was about this time that Shanahan approached Gibbs, who didn't want to be approached by anyone or anything, not even his faithful dog, Dog, whose name he chose because he couldn't think of any other and believed that animals should be called by their generic name.

"Sergeant, something big is coming and acting Sergeant MacKenna is the lynch pin in whatever it is," Shanahan said without any preliminaries.

MacKenna's name immediately brought Gibbs to full attention. "Big," he said, "and you say MacKenna is behind it?"

"I can't go into it any further, but the colonel should be made aware of it," Shanahan answered.

"I'll check with the colonel and give you a call," Gibbs said.

"I'll be in my office," Shanahan answered.

As soon as he left Gibbs' desk, Gibbs quickly riffled through the orders of the last few days, and quickly found Celenza's order promoting MacKenna to Sergeant First Class and making him Section Chief of the Heavy Weapons Section. The order predated the Colonel's order, which he also found, by a full twenty four hours. Knowing the regulation that stated a line company's needs in terms of personnel and equipment take precedence over a headquarters company, he also knew that more than a little skullduggery was involved in MacKenna's promotion. "All right," he shouted, "when I find out who's responsible for this fuck up, I'm going to nail his balls to the fucking barn door." And he stormed toward the colonel's office, entering without first knocking on it.

Miller, who had his head cradled in arms on the desk in a less than blissful sleep, almost fell out of his chair.

"We have a couple of serious problems," Gibbs announced waving the order in front of the colonel's face.

"We got more problems than 'Pennies from Heaven,'" the colonel answered sitting up in his chair behind his desk.

"Shanahan said 'something big' was coming."

"Big what?"

"He wouldn't tell me, but he said that you should be aware of it," Gibbs said.

"Now?" he asked looking at his watch. It was 06:30, and already there were more problems than there were at 02:30.

"MacKenna seems to fit—"

"Didn't I sign an order?"

"Yes, Sir. Here it is," and Gibbs placed it on the desk in front of him. "And here's Celenza's order that somehow you also signed promoting him to Sergeant

First Class and making him Section Chief of the Heavy Weapons Section."

Miller looked the two pieces of paper, or rather squinted at them before he shouted, "Get Shanahan in here on the double."

Gibbs went back to his desk, phoned Shanahan, and said, "The Colonel's office on double."

Shanahan's office was two doors away from the Colonel's, about three yards, and he practically fell over himself getting there. This was his opportunity to prove he wasn't the joke that Davidson thought he was.

The Colonel was waiting for him. "What's the big something that's coming?" he asked.

Shanahan winked and said, "Q clearance, sir."

The Colonel looked more confused than he usually looked and repeated the question.

Shanahan winked again and said, "Sergeant First Class MacKenna, Sir."

The Colonel's expression continued to express his confusion.

Shanahan nodded and winked again.

This wink was too much for the Colonel, and he asked, "Lieutenant is there something wrong with your left eye?"

"Why no, Sir."

"Then why are you winking it?"

"It sometimes happens, Sir."

"Very annoying," the Colonel said. "Better go see Fragola about it."

"Yes, Sir," Shanahan answered, anxious to escape.

But then the Colonel mumbled MacKenna's name and said, "I gave him to Gibbs."

"MacKenna," Shanahan echoed before he said, "He's with Baker Company."

Again the Colonel looked confused. "I know I signed a special order—Lieutenant, I want you to personally look into this. I don't like to have my men running around willy-nilly. It's not military, and with eight hundred new men it could cause a problem."

"Yes, Sir."

"He can't be in Able Company and headquarters at the same time."

"No, Sir."

The Colonel was becoming riled and that was not a good sign. Riled, he was totally unreasonable.

"When I sign a fucking order, I expect it to be obeyed, absolutely obeyed."

"Yes, Sir."

"Shanahan, I want to know why it wasn't obeyed and who the hell is this guy Private MacKenna?"

"Yes, Sir."

"I want answers. You have twenty-four hours, Lieutenant. Twenty four hours to prove yourself."

"Yes, Sir," Shanahan answered, aware of the newly placed load on his shoulders. The challenge he now faced made him feel more miserable than he felt before he went to Juarez.

The Colonel was about to dismiss him when the door opened and Gibbs entered the office, saw Shanahan, ignored him, and bellowed, "Celenza stole MacKenna."

"How the fuck did he do that?" the Colonel shouted back, his face as red as Gibbs'.

"His order predates yours," Gibbs said waving the two sheets of mimeographed paper in front of him. "There's been some shenanigans going cn and I'm not going to tolerate them."

"Shanahan," the Colonel yelled, "it's in your hands."

"Yes, Sir," was all he could say.

"Nobody steals one on my men," Gibbs growled. "MacKenna belongs to me."

Another knock on the door brought their attention to it.

"Come," the Colonel shouted angrily. Too many things were happening; and if Gibbs was right about shenanigans going on, he would be held responsible by Brigade for whatever happened; and Colonel Sides was on tough son-of-a-bitch.

Major Davidson entered the office and closed the door after him. A quick survey of who was already there, and he knew the reason for their meeting was MacKenna.

"What do you know about Sergeant—Private— that damn guy, MacKenna," Miller shouted.

"Sir," Davidson responded, buying a few moments to think of a logical answer, but not one that would compromise MacKenna's situation. "Colonel Sides might want MacKenna in Brigade," he said to avoid answering the question.

"Brigade?" Gibbs questioned.

"Holy shit, word does get around," the Colonel said. "If Sides wants him there's nothing we can do about it." Meaning, he wasn't about to cross swords with Sides over MacKenna, or for any other reason.

""Okay, now we sit tight and wait until a decision is made. Meanwhile, MacKenna stays with Celenza. Oh, and, Life Magazine is doing a photo spread of Sergeant MacKenna for their cover on their issue devoted to the Korean War. Their people will be around for a couple of days."

Gibbs's face was purple.

"Shanahan, you still have your mission," the Colonel said, adding, "Okay, this meeting is over."

* * *

Major Davidson went back to his office, closed the door and laughed until his sides hurt while Gibbs returned to his desk and sullenly stared off into space behind a steady stream of smoke coming from his pipe. And Shanahan, happy to be out of the Colonel's office, sat his bulk on the chair behind his desk and began to think of what might happen to him if he couldn't find who was responsible for the shenanigans that took place with regard to the Colonel's signed order. Korea was not where he wanted to be; the Department of Defense was his dream.

* * *

It was also the morning that Doctor Fragola scheduled a short arm inspection for the Battalion, starting with Able Company. Polly reminded Celenza of this shortly before he went out to inspect the Company, larger by two hundred men; none of whom had been issued arms because there were just enough pieces for the original compliment of men.

Celenza, like everyone else in the Battalion, suffered from lack of sleep that was compounded by his worrisome nature. He felt distinctly unmilitary. Not only was he afflicted with his hypochondria concerns but he was also having disturbing thoughts about Silvia and her question about *ménage à trois*. He wondered where that came from, even though she told him that Angie was the source. From his point of view the "fickle finger of fate" wasn't pointing at him; it was pressing down on him. But he couldn't luxuriate in self-pity. He had to go out and inspect his men.

"Polly, are there any special work details today?" he asked.

"No, Sir," came the answer.

Celenza nodded. "Ready, Carmine?"

"Yes, Sir," he said.

1st Lieutenant Thomas D. Celenza and First Sergeant Carmine Valdez left the hutment to carry out the Saturday morning ritual of inspection.

* * *

The previous night's experience with MacKenna gave Polly dual feelings: one of comradeship—after all, they had weathered a potentially difficult situation together—and his other reaction made him even more curious about the man. He was obviously either a very good Poker player or he could count cards. Perhaps he was a combination of both. And as for bluffing, he had never seen it done any better.

But there was something else playing in Polly's thinking: the niggling thought that Valdez and

Mastrangelo knew more about MacKenna than he did; that was especially true of Valdez.

Leeson's threat didn't seem to bother MacKenna; he accepted it as if he expected it and would have been disappointed if it hadn't been made. The more Polly thought about the exchange between MacKenna and Leeson, the more he came to believe that MacKenna was exactly the right man to solve his problem with Chester Trees.

* * *

When Celenza came face to face with MacKenna and snapped his piece from him, he was certain that MacKenna would know more about *ménage à trois* than any man in the unit. But the problem was how he could ask MacKenna about it without betraying his own ignorance. He returned the piece to MacKenna and moved on to the next man.

* * *

Doctor Fragola wasn't keen on doing a "short arm" inspection. It meant a few hours of looking at the men's cocks for signs of venereal disease, and because of the arrival of two hundred new men in the battalion, the inspection would take longer than it usually did. "Sick call" every morning except Sunday morning was bad enough, but a "short arm" inspection was intolerable because it took so much time away from his violin practicing. During the week he'd become an active member of the El Paso String

Quartet, and it was imperative for him to devote as many hours as possible during the day to practicing.

The men were ordered to drop their pants and wait until the doctor and medic were in front of them before exposing their cocks for inspection.

* * *

When the morning edition of the *El Paso Herald* arrived at Headquarters, the amount of shit that hit the fan was minuscule compared to the amount now flying around. The Colonel was being hammered by Colonel Sides, who was being blasted by General Gunner himself.

"I don't know where the information is coming from," Colonel Miller admitted.

"Well, fuck it man, you should know," Sides shouted. "You're in command of the unit, or aren't you?"

"I'm in command, absolutely, Sir," Miller said.

"Then get to the bottom of this mess. General Cannon will take over the command of Fort Bliss on Wednesday. I want this cleared up by the end of today, the latest by tomorrow. Understand?

"Yes, Sir," Miller said just as his other phone began to ring. He knew it was his bookie. He looked at the ringing phone longingly, but there was no way he could cut Sides off without giving himself another problem.

"I want fuckin' results from you," Sides yelled, "not Yankee bullshit."

"Yes, Sir."

"Over and out," said Sides.

"Roger that," Miller answered. Happy the conversation was over, he reached for the other phone and quickly dialed his bookie.

"There's a twenty to one running at Saratoga," his bookie said. "You want some of the action?"

"Put a hundred to win," Miller said.

"What's the name of the horse?"

"Constant Loser."

"That's not a good name."

"Yeah, but the fuckin' horse don't know that."

"I'm down for a C note," Miller said.

"Gotcha," the bookie answered and clicked off.

Miller ran his right hand over his face and glanced at his watch. It wasn't even 10 hundred, and he was already up to his eyeballs with alligators. With General Cannon in the offing, the future looked anything but good. He had heard at the officer's club that Cannon was worse than Gunner, and he was even more of a screamer than Gunner.

He left his chair, opened the door, and shouted, "Sergeant Gibbs, get Shanahan in my office on the double." Then he shut the door and went back to his desk.

Within two minutes, Shanahan was in front of him.

"You saw the morning newspaper?" Miller asked

"Yes, Sir."

"Well?"

"Well, what Sir?"

"Shanahan, there's someone in the Company doing us dirty, doing the Army dirty, doing the United

States of America dirty, and you, our S-2 ask me 'Well, what Sir?' "

Shanahan began to sweat again. He knew the moment that Gibbs told him that Colonel wanted him, that his day would be undone.

"This goes all the way up the chain of command and then back again to me and finally lands on you," Miller told him.

Shanahan looked bewildered.

"Lieutenant, there's a horse running at Saratoga this afternoon, and I put down a C note on him because the odds are twenty to one. It is a name that you should know, Constant Loser. Now the fucking horse doesn't know what that means; but you do, don't you?"

"Yes, Sir."

"I'm betting on you, Shanahan, to find the canary in the Company," Miller said. "I'm betting on you to find the guy who fucked up my orders. That's two bets Shanahan, and I want a double win, a win-win. Do you understand that Colonel Sides has a blow torch up his ass; and because he has one, I have one, and now you have one too."

"Yes, Sir,"

"Dismissed."

* * *

Doctor Fragola was almost done with the regular contingent of Able Company when he stopped in front of Private Gregory Giadono. The tell-tale leak was visible. Fragola nodded and said, "Burns like hell when you piss, soldier."

"Yes, Sir."

"Been ridin' bare back south of the border?"

Giadono didn't answer.

"I asked you a question, soldier," Fragola snapped. He was pissed. This stupid son-of-a-bitch in front of him would mean lots of paper work.

"Yes, Sir," Giadono answered.

"Contracting a venereal disease is a Courts Martial Offense," Fragola growled.

"Yes, Sir."

"Two steps forward," Fragola ordered.

"Now," he shouted, "everyone fucking clap for the son-of-a-bitch who has it."

* * *

After the previous night's experience, Polly decided to seek MacKenna's protection. He needed someone like him to deal with Chester Trees and his goons. The question was how much would it cost him? He already wanted him as a partner in his and Gibbs's shylocking business, but this would be more like a personal bodyguard. He figured a hundred a week might do it, but he was willing to go to one fifty.

As these thoughts took shape, he looked over to where Carmine was looking over the 201s of the new men assigned to them and wondered what he thought of the previous night's events so much so that he decided to ask him.

"He and Leeson will go at it again; you can be sure of it," Carmine said. "Leeson lost a lot of face, and that's something southern boys can't afford to do, especially to a Northern guy. It's serious business with them, a killing business to make it right, as far as they're concerned."

"But Leeson wouldn't know what he was tackling."

Carmine stopped what he was doing. "Do any of us really know anything more than MacKenna is one smart son-of-a-bitch and a damn good poker player?

"Card counter?"

Carmine shrugged. "Could be, but maybe he's both: a card counter and a damn good player."

Polly nodded.

Right now his problem wasn't MacKenna or Philip Trees; it was Gibbs, who was in a snit over the Colonel's decision to let MacKenna stay in Able Company. Knowing something about how Gibbs' mind worked, he knew that Gibbs thought he'd be able to snooker Celenza when the Review Board met to give their stamp of approval for the acting non-coms to be permanently appointed into the grade in which they were acting. There with a few well-chosen questions he could destroy MacKenna's credibility with. But that wasn't any of his concern. Right now Philip Trees held its center.

* * *

Shanahan rested his head on his two hands. He had a massive headache, and three APC pills weren't helping the situation. This time he couldn't escape to Juarez; this time he had to be visible.

Okay, he told himself, the 245th was mentioned, but there are over twelve hundred men in the Battalion and he had to narrow it down to one or two of them. One would be better.

He thought about all of the college graduates. There might be one or two in that grouping, a couple who were commies. And then he thought about MacKenna and Davidson. "One or both of them," he said out loud. "That could be the reason why Davidson has put a Q- clearance on MacKenna's two-oh-one file."

The idea didn't seem so farfetched; besides, it was the only one he had. To make his case, he'd need access to both their files, and he could only get that at the main base Personnel Section. He requisitioned a jeep and driver to take him down to the main base. The driver happened to be Mastrangelo, whose piece was declared dirty by Lieutenant Celenza, and as result was assigned to be "the standby driver" until eighteen hundred hours.

Mastrangelo was is a surly mood; he and his friend Salvator O'Mari were planning to spend Saturday afternoon and Sunday fucking their women in the house they rented on West side of Juarez. "Shit happens all the time when you're in Army," Mastrangelo told himself. But that didn't make him feel any better, and driving Lard Ass, made him feel worse.

Shanahan told Mastrangelo to wait for him, and he disappeared inside the base Personnel Building. He came up with William's file, but not MacKenna's. There wasn't a trace of him, nothing. Nada. Shanahan smelled the proverbial "rat;" in this case, a plant, a communist plant. Aware of how important this find was to his career, he almost shouted, "I got the son-of-a-bitch. I got him." But he didn't. Instead he snickered, making a sound more like a horse's nickering. Elated he left the building a half hour after he entered it and rejoined Mastrangelo in the jeep. "Ever drive Sergeant MacKenna anywhere?" he asked settling his bulk in the back of the vehicle.

"I drive anyone I'm told to drive," Mastrangelo said, sounding as surly as he could.

"Ever notice anything strange about him?"

Mastrangelo glanced back at his passenger. On general principles because he was an officer, Mastrangelo hated him. He hated him even more because he had a fat uncle who he hated and Shanahan reminded him of his fat uncle.

Shanahan repeated his question.

"All Sergeants are strange; that's what makes Sergeants," Mastrangelo said, starting the Jeep and beginning to move.

"I mean—"

"No, I never seen him whack off," Mastrangelo said, smiling as he continued to drive.

Mastrangelo's answer made him feel uncomfortable because that's exactly what he did earlier in the privacy of his office. He shifted his weight a bit, putting more of it on the left side of vehicle's railing. "Did he ever say anything political?" Shanahan asked, trying to cut to the heart of the matter that interested him.

"Sure, he said the fuckin' army stinks," Mastrangelo said, "and that all officers are shit heads."

Shanahan's face fired up into rosy red glow.

Mastrangelo said, "He's one smart cookie."

"Did he ever say anything against the government?"

"Sure."

"Do you remember what he said?"

"Something like it's a shit ass operation run by men who are crooks."

"He said that?" Shanahan asked gleefully.

"Yeah, he said lot of things in different languages too."

"Russian?"

"I only know Italian. I don't know from Russian."

Shanahan took a deep breath and slowly let it out. The wheezing made Mastrangelo again glance back at him. "You okay?" he asked, momentarily worried that if the Lieutenant was sick, he might have a real problem getting the bastard out of the jeep.

"Suppose I ask you—no, order you to report to me anything thing Sergeant MacKenna says—"

"Wait, a minute Sir," Mastrangelo said. "I ain't no stoolie."

"This is in the service of your country," Shanahan told him with as much brio as he could muster.

Mastrangelo, who practically lived in the streets of Williamsburg where he was born and raised, knew the ways of the streets, the code that guys like him lived by, and a stoolie was lower than a bed bug in that world. "I tell you what Lieutenant: I tell you only if it's Italian."

"But you understand English?" Shanahan said angrily.

"*Non capisco*" Mastranglo answered in Italian.

"Don't pull that Ginny shit on me," Shanahan growled.

Mastrangelo didn't answer, but when he came to a curve in the road he increased the speed of the jeep and turned the steering wheel so abruptly that Shanahan was forced to hold on to the side railing lest he be thrown to the other side of the jeep.

"What the fuck are you trying to do?" Shanahan shouted.

Mastrangelo shrugged and said, "No *capisco*."

"I'm going to report you," Shanahan said.

Mastrangelo laughed and continued to drive fast.

* * *

By 0930 Silvia and Angie were engaged in a phone conversation. Each of their husbands had called and had told them the RED ALERT had been cancelled, and that they would be home sometime later in the day, more toward evening than the early afternoon of the usual Saturday. Neither husband gave their respective spouses any reason for the delay. They just stated there would be one and let it go at that. The fact that Battalion had picked up four hundred additional men from the rail head was now in the realm of "classified information."

Though each woman was relieved their husbands weren't on their way to Korea, the false Red Alert made them realize that one of these nights it would be the "real thing" and they would be completely on their own, at least for the time they would remain in El Paso. But as soon as they returned to Brooklyn, they would be with their families again, especially the members of their immediate families, ready and willing to help and give advice. Their lives would be constricted; they would be treated more like widows than young mothers waiting for their men to return from the war. And if the unthinkable happened, their lives would be even more constricted; they would become perpetual widows with little opportunity, if any, to meet another man and marry him. In their society fealty to the dead was as strong as it was to the living; it was a culture into which they were born and raised. A woman functioning alone would be an easy mark for men without the protection of the family.

Silvia and Angie knew all of this; they had been raised on it by their respective families and subtly inculcated with it in the Catholic schools they had attended and had graduated from, which was why neither of them could let go of the possibility of becoming involved in a *ménage à trois* with F.K. Pulp or someone like him. Because it was forbidden, they wanted to eat of the delicious tree of sexual pleasure, and so they decided to meet in the afternoon in Alligator Park across the street from the El Paso Hotel at exactly the same time, 1300, that General Lewis Cannon was scheduled to land at Biggs Air Force Base; and though the two events seemingly had no connection, they eventually did have one.

* * *

At eleven hundred Ramblin' received a special delivery letter, the Subpoena from the HOUSE UN-AMERICAN ACTIVITIES COMMITTEE signed by its Chairman and witnessed by Roy Cohen, one of the Committee's lawyers. Ramblin' phoned F.K., who was in Las Cruses with his family.

"Got one too," F.K. said.

"Supposed to be there by Wednesday," Ramblin' commented.

"Isn't going' to happen that way," F.K. said. "One of my kid's birthdays is on Tues."

"We could fly up on Wednesday," Ramblin' offered.

"Unless I can jump out of a plane, I am not flying' in one. No, sir-ree, done had enough of that during the war. Besides, I've always had good luck on the Texas Eagle."

"Don't you ever think of anything else?"

"A good story and I got one."

"You sure as hell do."

"Why don't you and your Mrs. Come here, and we'll have one hell of a Mexican barbecue?"

"What the hell is that?"

"A clam bake with some steaks, hot dogs, sausages and whatever else the cook can find; and oh yes, a barbecued pig."

"How many people are you expecting'?"

"Could be a hundred, maybe two hundred. Some I know and some I don't. But there's one guy I want you to meet. He's an old friend of mine; we worked together in Italy during the war."

"I'll be there. What time?"

"You come when you come," F.K. answered. "It'll be goin' on for a long time."

"Around one, one thirty," Ramblin' answered, put the phone down and picked up a cigar from the humidor. A good, slow smoke is what he needed.

* * *

General Lewis's plane was told by the Air Control Officer to do "lazy eights" twenty miles out from Biggs Air Force Base, and to be careful not to stray into Mexican Air Space. The pilot rogered both directions and reported them to General Lewis by phone.

General Lewis was not a patient man, and demanded to know the reason for the hold up.

"No idea," the pilot answered.

"Well, Captain, you damn well better get an' idea and a fucking good one at that," Lewis shouted into the phone.

"Yes, Sir," the pilot answered.

Lewis glowered at his Aide d' Camp, General Latrin, also known by his subordinates as General Latrine.

"Sir, there are several battalions getting into position to welcome you," the pilot explained.

"Horse shit, I don't need or want a brass band," he yelled. "Tell those fuckers I'm comin' down," Lewis yelled. "Yes, sir, I'm comin' down."

"I can't land without clearance from the tower," the pilot responded.

"You need clearance, but I don't. Circle about ten miles from the field, and I'll jump," he said.

"Jump?"

"That's what I said," Lewis answered. "I got the certificate that says I can jump. So I'm going to jump."

General Latrin wasn't sure what his reaction should be; and while he was thinking about it, Lewis asked, "You coming with me?"

Latrin shook his head. "I haven't jumped in years. My certificate lapsed."

"Get me a chute," Lewis ordered.

Latrin knew that it would be useless to try to change Lewis's mind. Despite the fact that Lewis was a fit fifty year old man, jumping was not something he did every day. His fitness came from workouts in the gym and not from physical regimen that paratroops use to keep fit.

"I'm taking a walkie-talkie with me to let Headquarters at Bliss know where to pick me up," Lewis said, putting the chute on and adjusting its web straps to his fit.

The intercom-phone rang and Latrin picked it up, listened and said to Lewis, "There's a twenty knot wind blowing from the south-south-east.'

"So, what the hell does that mean?"

"You'll probably land close to Las Cruses."

"So?"

"The General says so," Latrin said, speaking into the phone.

"It's his game," the pilot answered, knowing it would be useless to try to tell Lewis he was risking his life. Generals don't appreciate being told they are fools or that they made a mistake. They are used to telling other people one or both of those things.

"Okay, I'm ready," Lewis said.

A few moments later, he stood by the opened door, holding onto its side, and with a wild cry of "Geronimo," he flung himself free of the airplane and began to count. When he reached one hundred, he pulled the rip cord. Nothing happened and he was still falling. He was more pissed than frightened. The ground seemed to be hurtling toward him. He groped for and finally found the rip cord for his emergency chute. He pulled it. The chute deployed and jerked him up so hard he was sure his arms were ripped out of their sockets. But they weren't and he quickly realized his descent had been considerably slowed. The wind was there as he had been told it would be, and it was taking him over some very rough terrain toward what looked like a large stand of pine trees. Within moments he crashed into one of the trees and blacked out.

* * *

"That's a damn parachute!" F.K. exclaimed to no one in particular, while holding a glass of cold Sangria in his right hand and looking up at the sky toward the South East.

His guests followed his lead and looked to that quadrant of the firmament where the chute was rapidly descending.

"Looks like he is headed for those pine trees," Ramblin' said, coming up to where F.K. was standing.

"He or she is goin' to break his damn neck 'ifin' they don't do some guidin'," F.K. said. "Been in situations like that a couple of time myself."

"He's done hit the trees," Ramblin' said. "Better go see if he's alive."

F.K., Ramblin' and a couple of the other men, the Sheriff of Las Cruses; Josh Lopez and Congressman, John White, from El Paso, took a jeep and drove the mile or so to where the chute was shredded by the branches of the pine trees.

At the end the chute they found the uniformed figure of General Lewis Cannon; he was swinging in the wind.

F.K. was able to shimmy up the trunk of the tree and grab hold of Lewis. "He's breathing," he yelled to the other men. "Seems like he's a fuckin' general; he's got two stars on his collar."

"Must be some damn expert on party crashin'," Ramblin' answered.

"How are we going to get him down?" Lopez asked.

"Very gently," F.K. answered. "He might have broken some bones."

"We'll need about forty feet of rope, at least a half inch thick," F.K. said. "I got some of that back at the house. One of you take the Jeep and fetch it."

"I'll go," White said.

"While you're there better call Bliss an' tell 'im what fell into our backyard, so to speak," F.K. said. "Somebody might be lookin' for him. His name tag says he's Lewis Cannon. Also, tell them to send an ambulance, a doctor and a couple of medics."

"Oaky," White said, easing the Jeep on to the nearby dirt road.

* * *

Silvia and Angie went to lunch in a small Tex-Mex restaurant not far from Alligator Park. They chose a table in the back of the place, away from the windows where someone they knew might see them and ask questions about they were doing in such a place, since the restaurant had an upstairs with rooms that served another purpose.

Without actually verbalizing their agreement to go upstairs, they agreed to find out what it would be like if they were involved in a *ménage à trois*. And Angie asked the maître d' how much a room would cost for an hour's use. He denied the existence of such rooms, but for two dollars he denied his denial and explained that a room for one hour with a shower cost eight dollars, increasing the price by three dollars for what he guessed were first timers and non-bargainers.

The required sum of money was given to him, and in return he handed Angie a key and told them to use the back stairway. The room was seedy and small. A queen size bed occupied most of it, and next to it was a night stand with a lamp without a lampshade and washbasin. There were two folded threadbare towels placed close to the washbasin. The shower was hidden behind a black plastic curtain.

The two women looked at each other with "now what" expressions of their faces.

"We've seen each other naked before," Silvia said, "so what's the difference now?"

Angie nodded and began to undress; and Silvia did the same.

As soon as they were nude, Silvia got on the bed taking the position near its head; and Angie occupied the foot. Both were on their haunches as they would have been if a man was under them.

Facing one another they giggled.

"Okay," Silvia said, "his mouth, tongue and maybe his fingers would be busily working on my cunt."

"His cock would be inside of me, and both of us would be moving," Angie said.

"That's right," Silvia agreed.

"But what would we be doing?" Angie asked, "I mean to each other."

"I don't know," Silvia admitted.

"Maybe, I'm just saying, maybe touching each other?" Angie suggested.

"Where, he was in you and—"

Angie reached out and put her hand on Silvia's breasts, lightly squeezing them. "Feels good?" she asked.

Silvia closed her eyes and placed the palm of her hands against Angie's breasts. "Feels, good," she said closing her eyes.

After a few moments their hands moved down each other's body, and they collapsed on to each other, doing to each other what Sister Olan told Silvia was a mortal sin to do to themselves. They changed their ministrations to each other from fingers to lips and tongues and experienced feelings neither of them could describe; their wordless sounds soon became muted cries of intense orgasmic pleasure. And when it was over and their breathing returned to normal, they held each other tightly. Both knew they would never again do what they had just done; unless, of course, there was a man involved. His presence would assure them that whatever they would do with each other was part of the game, nothing more. But they also understood they were connected in a way that most women weren't; and they had experienced and felt a love for each other that was totally different from what they felt for their husbands and children. Words weren't possible; and they kissed each other to express what they felt.

* * *

General Lewis experienced difficulty focusing. He saw branches of a tree, his chute, torn and twisted around other tree branches and he saw a man, a tall and lean one, smoking a cigar and wearing green shorts and a grungy looking tee-shirt with F.K. printed in bold letters on the front it. The man looked puckish to him; and he couldn't abide puckish looking men. They were trouble makers and the army could do without them.

The General's vision cleared, and he was indeed looking at a Puckish-looking man sitting on a limb not more than an arm's reach away from him.

"You're not dreaming, General. I'm real," F.K. said.

"Where the hell am I?"

"In a tree, about forty or so feet above the ground on my property."

"Who the hell are you?"

"F.K. Pulp, ace reporter and you are General Lewis Cannon, aka Loose Cannon by the men that you commanded."

"F.K. Pulp?"

"The very same," F.K. answered and blew three smoke rings.

Lewis frowned. "Your articles are—"

"Burning a few asses," F.K. said.

Lewis nodded. The guy was definitely puckish.

"Get me down," Lewis demanded.

"No can do," F.K. answered.

"Why the hell not?"

"Because you might have some broken bones or internal injuries."

"I'm fit as a fiddle," Lewis said.

"But you're not a fiddle, General. You're a mortal man, and crashing into one of my trees might have—"

"Nonsense, I didn't crash into anything. I was attempting to land and your fucking tree was in my way."

"Trees are not in the habit of walking or running when some idiot tries to land where they are," F.K. said blowing three more smoke rings."

"Did you just call me an idiot?"

"You're the guy who tried to land in my pea patch, aren't you?"

General Lewis grunted and repeated his request to be lowered to the ground.

"Patience, General. A whole damn fleet of ambulances and medics are on their way to rescue you," F.K. said.

"I don't have any patience. I want you to get me out of this tree now; do you understand that?"

"Perfectly. But it ain't goin' to happen," F.K. said smiling. "You're goin' to have to find some patience from somewhere."

"F.K. are you okay?"

"Sure am, Ramblin', and I'm having a real nice chat with General Lewis Cannon."

"You mean you got Loose Cannon treed?"

"Yeah, an' he ain't a happy man," F.K. said.

"Better come down before all the food is gone," Ramblin' laughed.

"No chance of that happenin'."

"Is he hurt any?" Ramblin' asked.

"Don't know."

"Who's Ramblin'?" Lewis asked.

"My boss, the publisher and owner of the newspaper I work for," F.K. said.

"I think I hear sirens," Ramblin' said.

"I hear them too," he said looking at Lewis, who indicated with a nod he heard them too. "Once you're down and you're declared to be fit as a fiddle, you can stay for the Mexican Barbecue; that's if you want to." F.K. offered.

Cannon made an inarticulate sound causing F.K. to say, "You ain't very mannerly, *mon General*."

"I'm not your General."

"Now I'd say that was damn lucky for you," F.K. laughed.

"F.K. you comin' down? Your guests are askin' fer you," Ramblin' yelled.

"I see White comin' up the road with two jeeps behind him and three ambulances followin' the jeeps."

"An' all for loose Cannon," Ramblin laughed.

"Must be worth somethin' more than I think he is," F.K. said. "I wouldn't give a plug nickel for the guy."

"I'm in no position to argue with you," Cannon said.

"You bet you're not," F.K. answered, "and when tomorrow's paper comes out, you'll be in worse position than you are now. You can bet on that." And he worked his way down to the ground just as White pulled up closer to him and Ramblin'.

* * *

It took some doing to bring the General down from his aerial perch, and using F.K.'s enormous kitchen as a makeshift triage center, the doctors who were dispatched with the Medics from Fort Bliss quickly ascertained that the General had two fractured ribs, many black and blue marks and several pulled ligaments, but nothing in the way of a bruised ego.

But there were other consequences to Loose Cannon's precipitous parachute jump. The Marching Band that was waiting at Biggs Air Force Base to welcome him was dismissed; and when General Gunner heard that his replacement had parachuted out of the plane rather than wait until it was cleared to land, he had a third Martini at lunch, which was enough to cause him to let out a wild whoop and shout, "Geronimo," then collapse from heart failure and subsequently be rushed to the William Beaumont

Army Hospital where his condition was declared serious, but not necessarily fatal.

There were also other consequences. F.K., through contacts at the Bigg's Control Tower, learned that the planes that caused General Cannon's delay were a half a dozen transports carrying wounded GIs from Korea to the William Beaumont Hospital, and that gave him the juice he needed for the story he wrote immediately after he hung up. And as a result of the General's departure, everyone at F.K.'s barbecue refilled their glasses with whatever they were drinking and Ramblin' made the following toast, "People who fall into other people's back yards, should at the very least have a drink with their surprised host or pay for the damages to his property, in this case one pine tree."

Glasses clinked, and everyone was the happier for having drunk another drink, except MacKenna. He was sitting on a lounge chair at one end of the pool thinking about his assignment. So far he had no real proof that Polly and Gibbs were loansharking. He had been told by several of the men that they were victims, but that wasn't enough. It wouldn't stand up as evidence in a hearing; and there was always the possibility that under questioning the victim would "button up," either out of embarrassment because he had to borrow from Polly or fear that some of Polly's and Gibbs' "friends" might send him to the hospital. In addition to the victims, MacKenna realized he needed something that would prevent them from "buttoning up." He had to get hold of the book in which the names of all of the victims were written and the sums of monies involved for each one of them. If he had the book, that would be one problem out of the way. The second problem was to find out who told F.K. about the nuclear tipped tracers, which lead to F.K. making a few very good guesses about nuclear ammunition and material that was being used somewhere in Fort Bliss. Since any of the information was Q Clearance material, that lead to the subsequent subpoenas for F.K. and Ramblin' by HUAC. At the moment neither problem was close to being solved.

"Are you finished staring at me?" the woman asked.

For a moment, MacKenna had no idea that she was speaking to him, but when he realized she was, he asked, "Was I?"

"You stripped me naked," she answered.

That wouldn't have been hard to do; she wore a two piece bathing suit with not much on bottom and just enough on top to cover her swollen nipples that were clearly visible through the bra's thin material. The rest of her was tanned. Most of her light brown hair was hidden under a white bathing cap, and she had green eyes.

"Now you're really giving me the once over," she said, and before he could answer, she asked, "Do I pass inspection?"

MacKenna laughed, "By the proverbial mile."

"Well, I don't know whether I should—"

"Take it as a compliment," MacKenna said. "But I wasn't really staring at you. I was hardly aware that you were where you are."

"Deep in thought," she said lifting herself out of the pool.

She was a long legged woman with a beautiful back and an ass like a small hillock. "Now you are staring," she said.

"I am indeed staring," MacKenna replied

She looked closely at him and said, "That's not your real face, is it?"

"No," he said quietly.

She removed her bathing cap and ran her hands through her hair; it fell below her shoulders. "I'm an artist," she said. "I paint portraits for a living."

MacKenna nodded. Though she was enticing, he wasn't sure that he wanted to continue the conversation. Her remark about his face put him off. It was too direct; he almost felt insulted.

"Very good plastic surgery," she said, "except for a few white scar lines that most people wouldn't notice."

"But you did," he snapped.

"Touchy, aren't you?"

"Not usually," he said. "But you came on like Gang Busters."

She laughed, "And with your staring, you didn't?"

"Touché," he said.

She sat on the edge of the chaise lounge without being invited and asked, "Were you in an accident?"

"You might say that," he said.

She waited for more of an explanation that he wasn't about to give. When she realized it, she said, "My name is Catharine Waters; I live up a ways from here, a few miles. F.K. owns ten thousand acres. My house is a couple acres off his property line."

"Technical Sergeant John MacKenna," he said, extending his hand to shake hers. "Newly assigned to the Two Hundred and Forty Fifth Infantry Battalion on Logan Heights."

"A Sergeant? She questioned, as if that was an impossibility.

"One more promotion and I'll have the three rockers; that will make me Master Sergeant," he said enjoying the confused expression on her face. She had obviously thought that he was someone important.

"What's your game, John?"

"Call me MacKenna, everyone does."

"Okay, MacKenna, I'll repeat my question. What's you game?"

Palms out, he lifted his hands. "Haven't got one," he said.

"Bullshit!"

"Honest."

"Guys like you always have a game."

"What kind of game do you think I have?" he asked. Exactly how she divined that he wasn't who he was pretending to be, he didn't know; but that she had, could be dangerous.

"I don't know, but I do know you have one," she said. "Maybe something to do with the nuclear stuff that F.K. has been writing about."

He smiled. She was far enough away from his real reason for being there, that he could afford to smile and let her interpret that anyway she wanted to. But he was sure she would take it as an affirmation of her guess.

"I'm hungry," she said. "What about you?"

"Yes, for two things."

"Oh?"

"Food and you.

"That's being blunt or sure of yourself."

"'Blunt, yes. Sure of myself, no. I could have misread your signs, signals if you will."

"Why don't we eat first and—"

"There's no 'and,' either we do or we don't," MacKenna said.

"What do you think?"

"We will."

"Let's go for the food first," she said.

"Only if dessert will follow?"

"Of course it will," she laughed.

* * *

General Cannon's aerial adventure was all but forgotten at F.K.'s Mexican barbecue. The guests were gorging themselves of the surfeit of food and drink; a few so much so that they found places to stretch out and fall in the deep sleep of the overfed and well oiled. But not Ramblin' and F.K.; they were holding court and enjoying every moment when MacKenna and Flo joined the circle around them.

"Ah, so you found each other," Ramblin' said. "I was wondering how long that would take."

"You might have saved some time by introducing us to each other," MacKenna said.

"I always let nature take its course," he answered, adding "Sometimes I give it a gentle nudge one way t'other."

"Unless it's in a laboratory, nature doesn't allow for much nudging."

"Living a life is like living in a laboratory," Ramblin's said. "You try a little of this or that and see what works for you." Then as afterthought, he added, "Most of our lives a 'jerry built,' and we hope was can hold them together."

"You goin' for the deep stuff, Ramblin'?" F.K. asked.

"Naw, the words just came to me and I had to let 'im out," he laughed. "I don't get involved in deep stuff; it's always too deep for me."

"What about you MacKenna, do you get involved in 'deep stuff?' "

MacKenna knew everyone was looking at him and wondering who the hell he was. "I'm not sure what you mean by 'deep stuff,' " he said.

"The big questions, like why are we here, or why do we have good and evil? Stuff like that," F.K. said.

"I intend to think about them in my old age," MacKenna answered. "But right now I have other things on my mind." And he circled Flo's waist with his left arm, his thumb resting below her left breast.

"That's somewhat obvious," he laughed.

The conversation moved to the subpoenas F.K. and Ramblin' got, and what they intended to do about them.

"We're going to Washington, and expect a very warm reception," Ramblin' laughed.

"Hot would be more like it," F.K. said.

"Or very cold," Ramblin' offered.

"Makes no matter," F.K. said. "We'll speak our bit and that will be that."

"I'm plannin' to enjoy myself and do a bit of sightseeing; maybe even get to New York and see a couple of shows. I haven't done that in a few years," Ramblin' said.

"That's about the way I see it," F.K. added.

"Just watch out for the sharks," MacKenna warned.

"We don't plan to go near the water," Ramblin said.

Everyone laughed, except MacKenna who had dealings with the committee—and Roy Cohen and the committee's lawyer.

* * *

Polly and Carmine spent the entire time going over the new men's records and writing requisitions for forty more cots, mattresses, sheets and blankets. It was boring, detailed work; and when one or the other stopped to stretch or run over to the mess hall for a cup of coffee, the other one had time to think about the events of the previous night.

As far as Polly was concerned, MacKenna and Leeson would eventually have to fight it out, and though MacKenna was "a cool cat," Leeson had the weight and the reach. He wouldn't bet on MacKenna, but he'd make book on Leeson if it came to a showdown between the two of them. Thinking about it that way, gave him the idea of actually setting up a betting operation based on which one of them wins, either by a knock out or by saying, *he's had enough.* He and Gibbs would set the odds, and the betting would start at a dollar and top out at ten. He'd have to talk to Gibbs about it first before doing anything. He couldn't go it alone; Gibbs was the money man. But Gibbs was definitely in a snit over Celenza besting him in their grab for MacKenna; and now Lard Ass was involved, though Polly thought that Shanahan couldn't find a woman's cunt even if her legs were wide open and he was looking at it. Still, he just might get lucky, and if Polly knew, he'd be in deep shit with Gibbs, to say nothing about what the Command might do to him. Whenever he asked himself, which was seldom, why became involved in such schemes, the answer was always the same: for the fun of it, or if money was involved, to beat the other guy. Suddenly, he had a brilliant idea, one that he could make Lard Ass dance for. He'd just hint to him that MacKenna was slightly pink. That would get rid of him and Gibbs wouldn't fret over the fact that MacKenna wound up under Celenza's command. But that bit of *playfulness* would have to wait until after the show down fight between MacKenna and Leeson that had to come.

In the meantime, Polly had his own problem to worry about: *how to avoid getting the shit knocked out of him by Deets' goons* the next time he encountered Deets and his heavies in Manelos or, for that matter, anywhere else. Of course his friends would always be with him, except when he was with... But they weren't the kind of bruisers that Deets employed. They were Pros. They knew how to inflict pain. It was at best a melancholy thought, and put a damper on his previous thinking.

Whenever Carmine took a break from the monotony of work that mainly consisted of checking Polly's work, which was usually accurate, all he had to do was sign off on the requisitions, and place them on Celenza's desk for him to sign off as the Company's Commanding Officer. Carmine also thought about the events of the previous evening and was more convinced than ever that MacKenna wasn't just a "dog faced" GI. But he had no way of proving it, and wasn't even sure that he wanted to prove it. After all, it didn't make any difference to him what MacKenna was as long as he kept his section running in good order. But he was sure that Leeson would be gunning for him. And he was also sure, despite their differences in weight and reach, MacKenna would give a good account of himself. But if Leeson's buddies were there and MacKenna was wining, they would be sure to help Leeson; then, MacKenna wouldn't have a chance in hell to come out of the fight without serious damage. He decided he wasn't going to let that happen. Exactly how he was going to stop it, he didn't know, but he was sure he'd think of away.

* * *

MacKenna and Flo left the barbecue for a couple of hours and went to her place, a native stone-built hacienda styled place that sat on a bluff overlooking an all but dried out stream, which, she assured him turned into a raging torrent when the rains came. He believed her. He would have believed anything she said because in the aftermath of their voracious sex, he found himself in the luxurious afterglow of sexual satisfaction and exhaustion.

It was the time when they could tell one another about their pasts, but neither one went deeply into the darkness of that place. He mentioned that he was a widower, that his wife had been killed in an automobile crash a few years back, and she told him she had been previously married to money and now was divorced, doing what she had wanted to do all her life: paint.

He found her physically enchanting, with lovely crescent-shaped breasts, tipped with generous dark pink nipples. And she unstintingly gave herself to him, giving him the opportunity to sexually play her as if she was a deep throated cello. Hemingway wrote that for Maria the earth moved when she and Robert made love for the first time. For MacKenna the earth stopped; and for a few deliciously exquisite moments it stood still, and he was "where Alph the sacred river ran through caverns measureless to man ..." where he glimpsed the crystal beauty of the Earth and the sky wedded in a seamless continuum of which they were simultaneously a part of and not a part of. And when they were finally done and were a tangle of arms and legs; she held his cock between her breasts and he rested his head on her black haired mons Venus. "It would be easy to mistake this for love," he said.

And she answered, "Is that what you want to do?"

He laughed. "Is that what *you* want to do?"

"No fair, answering a question with a question," she said.

"We've watered the garden; let's see what grows."

"An interesting way of putting it, but a garden needs constant care."

"To be sure," MacKenna said. "I promise you I'll give it the care it needs."

"I believe you," Flo said.

CHAPTER VII

On Sunday Shanahan took Communion and immediately afterwards went to his office. As far as he was concerned, the Colonel didn't understand that MacKenna's connection to something bigger than the fuck-up that failed to transfer him from Celenza's Company to Gibbs's section. There was no doubt in Shanahan's mind that MacKenna was the point man for a nuclear transition for the 245th; but no matter how hard he tried to connect the dots, that would prove he failed to do it. Even to his own men, MacKenna was a mystery man. Then it struck him like Aphrodite exploding out of Zeus's brain, he came to the conclusion that MacKenna was a Russian agent placed there to steal nuclear secrets, and what was just as horrific was Major Davidson aiding and abetting a Russian agent. Now he was able to see all of the dots and how they connected one to another.

With a big smile on his face, he inserted a piece of paper and the necessary carbon papers and flimsies to make three copies in the typewriter in front of him and centered it before he typed: A CONFIDENTIAL REPORT ON THE ESPIONAGE ACTIVITIES OF TECHNICAL SERGEANT JG MacKENNA and MAJOR JOSEPH DAVIDSON IN THE 245th INFANTRY BATTALION, FORT BLISS, TEXAS. He removed that piece of paper, inserted another set of paper, carbons and flimsies and began to type.

With Aristotelian logic he developed his argument and twenty pages later he concluded it with "Eternal Vigil Is the Price of Democracy," then typed in his name, his serial number and his MOS, and signed it. Satisfied, he locked the document in a drawer and went to Juarez to celebrate.

* * *

Both women—Silvia and Angie—were full of remorse for their "un-natural" acts and were overly solicitous of their husband's sexual needs, hoping that their actions and the pleasure they gave and received would propitiate their restiveness. Both told themselves that what had happened was "an accident," and wouldn't happen again, even if they were involved in a *ménage a tois*. But neither one was sure of their resolution. They knew how quickly "things" could get out of control. And thinking about it wasn't making it any easier to rid themselves of their guilt, and even worse was the niggling thought in the remotest, darkest corner of the their brains that they had immensely enjoyed themselves, and that with a man present it would be even more fun and the pleasure more intense.

They were in such a quandary that each took time to go to confession, hoping that by telling someone about their experience it would release the pressure building in them to confess their transgression to their respective husbands, which they knew would cause monumental explosions in Italian, causing words to be hurled about like thunderbolts, and followed, perhaps, by physical punishment.

But each of the priests that heard their confession was so sexually stimulated, they masturbated; and appalled not only at what they heard but also by what that they did, each demanded the confessor meet with them for private instruction hoping it would lead to a sexual encounter that would, they would assure their apostates, lead them to a state of grace in the eyes of "the Son, the Father and the Holy Ghost."

Both women agreed to accept such instruction as the priest would give, and left the confessional booth with tears of thankfulness streaming down their cheeks.

* * *

But most of the men of the 245th Infantry Battalion on base were commandeered by their First Sergeants to help with the unloading and distribution of additional cots and mattresses for the additional four hundred men. Hutments built for four men were reconfigured to hold six men and in a few extreme situations eight men. The work was hard and because the temperature was in the upper nineties, it was sweaty and exhausting as well. By mid-afternoon, everything that could be done that day was done, and the men were free to leave the Company Area.

All of the new men, having heard about the delights offered in Juarez, went there in groups of three, five and ten men. All of them having been paid before leaving Fort Hood had collectively thousands of dollars to spend in Manelo's, which was highly recommended by the men of the 245th.

* * *

Though it was Sunday, Philip Trees was there with three of his goons looking for Polly, who was also there, but with a woman in one of the back rooms. He couldn't wait any longer for the "opportune moment" to approach MacKenna. One had past, and another one might not come down the road, so to speak, for several days. Meanwhile, he was becoming hornier and hornier as the days passed, and he wanted to keep track of the traffic in Manelo's; it was his dream to buy a piece of it. But so far every time he mentioned the idea to Gibbs, Gibbs became Saint Gibbs and would not consider having a conversation about what he called, "tainted money."

By passing out a few ten dollar bills to the various bar tenders and Manelo's own watch dogs, Philip learned that Polly was in Room 609, one of four rooms reserved for special guests. He'd fucked more than one prostitute in that room. His first impulse was to barge in and beat the shit out of him in front of the woman. But then he realized that Manelo would not take kindly to the possibility of the room being wrecked, and just become angry enough to send his own people in who were all too handy with knives. The combination of knives and his three guys with guns was not a good one; there would be casualties. He might be one of them. Polly was well liked at Manelo's. These thoughts stopped Philip from taking immediate action, and gave two of the waiters, who happily took Philip's ten spots, time to warn Polly that Philip was there with three of his sharks.

Polly, who would walk the proverbial mile to avoid a fight, decided that now was as good a time to have one as any; since the fight was inevitable. What

Polly had no way of knowing was that MacKenna and FK Pulp were at the bar. FK was scheduled to leave on Monday at 1200 hours on the Texas Eagle, and MacKenna, who had spent Saturday night with Flo, had wandered into Manelo's for a quiet drink and to think about how emotionally involved he wanted to become with Flo. It was something wonderful to have glorious sex with a woman, but a very different thing to develop feelings that go beyond lust.

FK was there for a very different reason; he was hoping to pick up more information about the 245th's involvement with the nuclear program, if it was involved at all and Manelo's was where the unit's men went when they were in Juarez. And a few drinks sufficiently loosened them up for FK to ask seemingly innocent questions and come up with interesting answers. So, each of them had their particular reason for being in the same place at the same time thereby eliminating the element of coincidence. And since they were friends, it was natural for them to be drinking together because that was what friends did.

When Philip Trees walked in with three of his bully boys, FK pointed him out to MacKenna, whose reaction was noncommittal, except that "his friends look the type." Then they turned their attention to FK's imminent appearance before the HUAC Committee. FK wasn't in the least bit fazed by the subpoena, "nor is Ramblin'," he said. "We'll make a hash out of it, you can be sure of it."

"I'll drink to that," MacKenna said, touching his glass of bourbon to FK's.

Manelo himself came into the room. A short man, with many gold crowns on his teeth and wearing a white western cut suit and shirt and black sting tie and large sombrero, he looked more like a comic character than the owner of a very successful restaurant and brothel. He spotted FK and immediately joined him and MacKenna, introductions followed and handshakes and Manelo called over to the bartender for "another round of drinks for my friends and soda water and twist of lemon for me."

"So, FK how you goin' to beat the rap they got set up for you in Washington?" Manelo asked.

FK laughed, "That, Amigo, is a secret. If I tell you, it won't be a secret anymore."

"You got some set of *cajones,* Manelo said, toasting FK with his soda water and twist of lemon.

Manelo didn't seem at all interested in MacKenna until he turned his attention to him and asked, "You civi or sojor?"

"Soldier, Tech. Sergeant 245th Infantry Company - -"

"Ah the nuclear guys!"

MacKenna laughed, but said nothing.

Manelo joined him; then, he said, "One day we all go puff and become a cloud."

MacKenna looked at FK, "Don't believe everything you read."

"Only the good stuff," FK said; then spotting Polly coming out into the main room from behind a black velvet curtain, he said, " Head's up, trouble."

Polly hesitated for a moment, and then walked into the room with his "friends;" one on either side of him and the other bring up the rear.

"Philip's bullies are packing," FK said. "They always do."

"How do we do this?" Mackenna asked.

FK smiled and said, "The easy way.'

Manelo said nothing.

Philip and his bullyboys moved toward Polly, while FK and MacKenna grabbed hold a couple of bottles on the bar and with exacting aim hurled them at two of Philip's guys, the third turned toward them only to get a third bottle crashing to his forehead. With the three of them down, MacKenna disarmed one, FK the other one of Manelo's men took care of the third.

The action was so fast that Philip didn't know what happened until he was standing in front of Polly and realized the room was suddenly steeped in silence and neither of his bullyboys was at his side.

Manelo went up to Philip and said, "You got big trouble, understand?"

Philip nodded.

"Tell me, 'I got big trouble'. I want to hear it."

"I got big trouble," Philip said.

"Okay, we fix," Manelo said. "You pay Polly five G's for damages."

"What damages?" Philip asked.

"What kind of trouble you have?"

"I have big trouble," Philip answered.

"Okay, you understand. Five Gs an no more shit from you, or I'll have you *cajones* cut off and sent to your father. Understan? An' if the check bounces, I bounce you off a couple of walls so you un'stan' how rubber feels."

Philip nodded. He was very pale.

"You don't look so good," Manelo said. "Go over to the bar, have a couple of drinks; then go in the back and have Lilly give you a blow job. You'll feel much better. As for your guys, they can get a couple of free drinks; but if they want pussy, they have to pay for it. For you, it's free this one time because before you leave, you goin' to write a check for 5Gs and give it to her. Make it out to me, Manelo. I give it to Polly after I take my cut."

"Pure justice," FK said. He and MacKenna were back at the bar.

"Lovely to watch," MacKenna said.

"I'm hungry," FK said. "How about a steak?"

"I'll go for that," MacKenna answered.

* * *

Polly was too stunned by the rapidity of the events to do anything more than experience them in the kind of slow motion that the human brain is capable of producing in moments of crises. It was only when Manelo took hold of him by his arm and said, "Amigo you too need a drink." And leading him to the bar, he ordered the specialty of the house: a mixture or Tequila, Bourbon, and pure Russian vodka, a dash of Scotch and a twist of lemon.

The concoction had an immediate effect on Polly; it brought him back to reality just at the time that Manelo said, "My cut is four Gs. I give you one G because you get me four."

"Two Gs," Polly said.

Manelo counted with, "I got to consider the damage."

"What damage?"

"Ah, there's where you're missin' it," Manelo said. "The damage that could-a happened."

"But it didn't happen," Polly protested.

Manelo wagged a ringed figure at him. "I see broken tables, chairs and a smashed mirror, maybe even a couple of dead bodies, and dead bodies no good for business, even the pussy business falls for with dead bodies layin' around."

Polly couldn't think of a way of arguing Manelo out of another G; besides whatever he was drinking was making him sleepy and horny at the same time. Despite these two incompatible feelings, he realized he'd learned that imagination can be, if used the way Manelo was using it, a money maker.

* * *

By the time General Cannon saw the Sunday edition of the *El Paso Times*, it was early afternoon. His recent stunt caused him to sleep later than he usually did. He was by nature and early riser, and the requirements of command demanded an eighteen hour day, if for no other reason than the various social functions he attended in order to promulgate his name in Washington.

FK's article with accompanying photographs of him in the tree and then on the ground, began with the headline: "FORT BLISS'S NEW COMMANDER MAKES A CRASH LANDING IN A PINE TREE."

FK spared him nothing. He referred to him as "the quintessential party crasher or the point man for a new trend in the old game of party crashing.

General Loose Cannon was too impatient to wait until transports carrying wounded men from Korea landed at Biggs Air Force Base, and made the unique decision to land by parachuting, a stunt that was to have been a grand gesture of command ability turned out to be something like a 'Partridge in a Pear tree.' But the General isn't a partridge and the tree he wound up in wasn't Pear Tree, it was a Pine Tree on my property.

"Ordinarily, whenever I have a Mexican Barbecue, I get some weird types - - professional party crashers. But the General doesn't fall into that category. His escapade was nothing more than a blatant example of poor judgment that went so far as to claim his crash in one of my pine trees was the fault of the pine tree; seeing it was him, the tree should have pulled itself up by its roots and moved out of the way.

"Such is the hubris of those to whom we entrust the lives of our people in the military; such is the new commander of Fort Bliss, Texas."

CHAPTER VIII

F.K. bordered the TEXAS EAGLE on Wednesday morning, and was unable to buy anything better than a Coach Ticket, which meant he would be sitting all the way to Washington. He could have gotten a roomette if he gave money to the right people. But roomettes, as far as he was concerned, were okay when the bed was up during the day; at night with the bed down they reminded him of the small cell he was forced to occupy for several uncomfortable days after the German's captured him just outside of Paris before the city fell to the Allies. At that time, he was almost certain he would be executed but luck intervened and he was rescued by a squad of Tommies, who happened upon the house where he was incarcerated, saw there were Jerries inside and decided to kill or capture as many of them as they could. They wound up killing half of them and took the other half prisoners. Such memories were better left in the nooks and crannies of his brain rather than have them leak out into the reality of the present, so he accepted the ticket for the Coach without so much as a grimace and settled on a seat next to three GI's on their way to New York for a thirty day leave before shipping out to Korea.

The soldiers occupied two long seats that faced each other. Between the seats and the racks above them they stowed their belongings. They were men in their early twenties. All of them were from the New York area. Julian, a tall thin man, was the oldest - twenty two. Terry was twenty and James was nineteen. Julian had his sergeant's stripes; the other two were Corporals.

F.K. found them funny, and totally clueless to what awaited them when they finally arrived in Korea. But he wasn't about to tell them and perhaps spoil their leave. War, for all the theories about it, was in the end "a hands on experience."

Because they were in the Coach section of the train, they were not permitted to enter the dining car, whose amenities were limited to those passengers with room or roomette tickets. The passengers in the coach section either bought food with them or they purchased it along the way whenever the train made one of its many whistle stops. But F.K. wasn't about to abide by the railroad's rules, and when James announced he was hungry and the other two men agreed that they too were hungry, and F.K. felt that he'd enjoy a bowl of soup and a sandwich, or perhaps a hamburger with a slice of onion and lettuce and tomatoes, he said to his young companions, "Follow me."

The four of them headed for the Dinning Car, but as soon as they approached it, they were stopped by a Conductor, who asked to see their tickets.

"No problem," F.K. said, handing the man a twenty dollar bill. "That should cover any questions until these young men reach New York."

Expressionless, the conductor nodded.

Inside the Dinning Car, they were greeted by the Maître de, who immediately informed them that there weren't any tables available.

"That's odd because I see three," F.K. said.

"They're reserved," the Maître de said.

"Suppose I told you that one of those tables is reserved for me and my guests," F.K. said, speaking softly and earnestly.

"And your name is?"

"F.K. Pulp."

The Maître de consulted a sheet of paper on a clipboard before he said, "I'm sorry, Sir your name isn't on my list."

F.K. rubbed his chin; and still speaking softly, he said, "Let's not fuck around. There are three empty tables and my three companions and I are going to occupy one of them and be served. It's either that, or I'll inform the diners already here that you are denying seating to soldiers who will soon be going to Korea. I don't think they would appreciate that, and neither would your boss whoever he is."

The Maître de hesitated.

"Try me," F.K. said.

"Gentlemen, please follow me," the Maître de said.

Once they were seated, everyone in the dining car turned to look at them.

"They're wondering who we are," F.K. said, adding, "Smile at them, that'll confuse them even more."

* * *

Their lunch was a success and they left the table with the feeling of comradeship among them. F.K. regaled them with off-color jokes and stories, none of which had the slightest connection to the war in which he served. Though memories of that war came back despite his efforts to suppress them, so by the time the four of them returned to their seats in the coach car, his mood was considerably less jocular, and he pretended to sleep rather than engage in conversation.

There was one memory that, like a spoiled child who demands to be heard will throw a tantrum, continued to swirl in his consciousness. He was working with a group of Italian partisans in Italy north of Bolzano, in the pre-Alps and they had a running battle with German Alpine Troops in which they suffered heavy casualties. But they managed to capture a Colonel and several of his aides, who were summarily executed. The Colonel, who was tied to a tree, witnessed the executions without as much as a blink when shots were fired.

By that time in the war, F.K. killed, mostly at close quarters, many times. But now the Commander of the Partisans handed him a bayonet and said, "He's yours."

F.K. knew he was being tested. And he also knew he needed the trust of the men if he hoped to complete his mission, which was to intercept a train headed for Germany and packed with Italian Jews. As soon as they were liberated, they would be taken to the Swiss border; and once across it they would be free.

F.K. remembered it was very quiet. He walked up to the Colonel, whose very dark gray eyes were riveted on him. Neither one spoke, though F.K. was fluent in German and Italian, with more than a smattering of French and Spanish at his command.

It was very cold and both their breaths steamed and co-mingled in the frigid air.

"Do it," the Commander said.

F.K. glanced at him. He was a medium sized man, wore a sheepskin coat, a woolen cap that covered his ears and carried an American made M-1 rifle. Before the war, he was a Professor of History at the University in Turin. Now there was a price on his head that was challenging him to kill "in cold blood," something he'd never done before.

He remembered giving the Commander a slight nod, and turning to the Colonel, he jammed the bayonet into his heart. For an instant his body stiffened, then went limp. He was dead.

* * *

At the same time F.K. boarded the TEXAS EAGLE, Ramblin' boarded a charted DC3 with an entourage of several people, including the Mayor of El Paso and Juarez, Worth, and four Mescalero Apache Indians, one of them, a tribal chief. All of them were character witnesses for him.

He had reserved a block of rooms in a hotel in the Rock Hill Section of nearby Virginia. Far enough away from the capital to escape from its hurly-burly atmosphere after the day's hearing was ended. He expected the hearing to last at least two days, maybe three. But he figured that it might take him and F.K. more than one day to wreck the hearings. He was not going to let the Committee "ride rough shod" over him as it had done to so many others who were summoned by it. The Chairman's blatant misuse of his power and his open disregard for an individual's constitutional rights had to be stopped and he felt a powerful callin' to do just that; and he knew that F.K., despite his sexual escapades, felt the same callin'. It was somethin' profoundly religious at its core, or maybe it superseded religion because it concerned the future of the country's citizens and their right to speak and write without fear of being harassed or arrested by local or Federal authorities.

* * *

This was also the afternoon for the big review to welcome General Lewis Cannon, the new Commander of Fort Bliss. For the occasion, two unrelated events took place though one of them had a profound effect on the other. The first, an anomaly of nature, a temperature spike to one hundred and ten degrees; and the second, the formation of eighty-two thousand men in marching order waiting to step off.

Every soldier knows that time in the army has two components: yesterday and hurry up and wait. When something is to be done immediately, yesterday applies; but when something is to be done that lacks a real or imagined urgency, it's always a hurry up and wait condition, which was why eighty-two thousand men were formed up at ten hundred when the parade was scheduled for thirteen hundred.

Every soldier also knows that generals are always late for their own parades. This practice has a long history that goes back to pre-Mosaic times, a fact of absolutely no interest to the several thousand men who were waiting for General Lewis. Their collective interest was to get the fucking thing over with as soon as possible.

Because the 245th was not an artillery unit, it was relegated to the end of the very long column of men by a special order from General Mortar, who was happy that Lewis would have to deal with the problems created by someone in the unit. But the men of the 245th were, like the rest of the men in the formation, not only drilled under the blazing sun, but they were also without water. Colonel Miller decided they would look a lot "smarter" without canteens dangling from their web belts. Though the men were issued salt pills at breakfast, which was still half of their usual ration, and urged to drink as much water as possible, by 10 hundred several of the men passed out and the Medics carried them off the parade ground to the shelter of a tent, where Doctor Fragola applied the necessary remedies for heat exhaustion.

Celenza was having difficulty focusing on the first rank of Able Company; the men became wavy, and though he distinctly heard himself order the men to *straighten out* nothing happened. The men were still wavy, and then he felt that he was falling down a coal chute.

"Medic," Semelinsky shouted. "Medic. The CO is down."

Before the Medics got to Celenza, MacKenna dashed forward from his position in front of the Heavy Weapon Section; and grabbing hold of the Lieutenant, he placed him across his back in the fireman's position, carried him to the Medic's tent and left him in Fragola's hands.

Though the entire episode took only two or three minutes, it was long enough for Celenza to say, though he was delirious, "*Ménage à trois* and nuclear bullets. Silvia, I'm innocent." MacKenna heard what he said, and from it knew he would soon have one of his problems solved.

Before he returned to his former position, he drank liberally from the Medic's lister bag at Fragola's invitation. Standing in front of his section, MacKenna tried not to think about how hot it was and thought about Flo. He hadn't seen or spoken to her since Sunday morning and—

Something began to happen; he saw the dust rise far in front of him and knew that the parade had begun. He glanced at his watch: it read 1400. By the time the 245th stepped off it would probably be closer to 1700, and many more men would wind up in the Medic's tent. But at the same time something else was beginning to happen some distance out in the desert and along the mountain tops to the north and west of Fort Bliss. Small swirls of sand were lifting their cones off the sun baked desert floor and very large thunderheads were positioning themselves on the high escarpments of the mountains. No one saw what was happening in the desert, but some of the men in the various formations whose biology and physiology were sensitive to atmospheric pressure changes began to feel even more uneasy than they previously had.

Vinny was one of those afflicted with such sensitivity, and his attention was drawn to the clouds on the mountains which were now a mixture of gray and white. Since the men were standing at rest, rather than at ease, it permitted them a certain amount of movement, three or four steps in any direction from their assigned place. Vinny took it upon himself to approach Second Lieutenant Richard Dix, the ninety day wonder who was the officer in charge if the Heavy Weapons Section and was obviously terrified by MacKenna's knowledge of the weaponry under his command.

Dix, who had a choirboy look, was having the same difficulty coping with it as everyone else, and looked at Vinny as if he was looking at the man through the wrong end of a telescope.

"Sir," Vinny began when he was close enough to Dix to speak, "we're in for a change of weather, a violent one, if you ask me."

"Is that so, sergeant? And just where did you get the information from?" the lieutenant asked.

"I can feel it, Sir. I always can feel a weather change."

"Tell me it's going to snow, and I might be happy."

"See those clouds over there," he said, pointing to the mountains where the clouds had changed from white and gray to dark gray and practically black.

"So? The sun is still shining here," Dix said.

Vinny couldn't deny that.

"Besides, the clouds build over the mountains on most days because of the cooler air up there," Dix explained.

"Yes, Sir," Vinny said, and he returned to his place in the formation.

But MacKenna who was a few paces from Dix couldn't help but overhear his conversation with

Vinny, and found himself agreeing with him. The clouds on the mountain tops weren't their usual puffy white; they were dark, almost ugly and certainly threatening.

* * *

General Mortar and General Lewis, and their respective wives, families and aides, were seated in the reviewing stand watching the parade pass. The generals and their aides saluted the colors wherever they passed, and returned the "eyes right" salutes of the marching men with quick "high balls" of their own.

General Lewis was still smarting from F.K.'s article about him in the Sunday newspaper, and the two pieces that followed characterized him as someone akin to General Douglas MacArthur, whose aide he had been before MacArthur retired and gave his "old soldiers never die, they just fade away" speech to both houses of Congress.

On the other hand, General Mortar was absolutely gleeful over F.K.'s articles, though he absolutely detested the man because of the mess he created with his nuclear ammunition stories, where more than a few of his guesses were close enough to the truth to give the Russians and the Chinese good reasons to think long and hard about what he had written. But like Lewis he had good friends in Washington, a couple on the HUAC Committee ready and waiting to pounce on F.K. and his publisher Ramblin'.

Generals don't appreciate having their parades rained on. Lore that goes back to Greek and Roman times, views an unhappy event as an omen for worse things to come. Rain or snow on the day of the parade tends to dampen, if not diminish the ego of this select group of military men, who have it within their power to send tens of thousands of men into the hellish realism of combat with often nothing more than their egos to back up their decisions.

But this time, on the parade ground of Fort Bliss, Texas, a sudden, but powerful wind came up and blew away the canopy over the reviewing stand, jagged flashes of lightening tore across a black sky followed by booms of thunder and golf ball sized hailstones fell, pummeling everyone on the stands and all of the marching men and those waiting to march. Neither the generals nor the marching men could hold their positions. The parade was a disaster and General Lewis brooded about the underlying significance of the event, while General Mortar celebrated it by drinking several shots of scotch before his evening round of Martine's.

* * *

At two o'clock El Paso time, Angie put through a phone call to her parents in Brooklyn, and complained to them that Vinny wasn't getting enough to eat in the army because new men had come into the unit and there wasn't enough food for everyone.

Around the same time that Angie was talking to her parents, Silvia was also speaking to her parents about the short ration situation in the 245th. Neither woman mentioned their recent sexual "awakening," nor did they say anything about the "instruction" they would soon receive from their priests.

At the end of their conversations, their respective mothers said to their husbands that something had to be done to alleviate the shortage of food that their son-in-laws were experiencing. The result of these conversations led to Thomas' father and Vinny's father meeting and discussing the situation. That, in turn led to a sit down with Louie, the Tiger, whose eyes watered when he heard about the hardship that the men of the 245th had to endure; but at the same time, he saw the possibility to pull off a wonderful scam that would enrich "the organization" by a couple of mil, and make him look real good in the eyes of Little Nick, who headed the "Organization" on the eastern seaboard.

With the promise to do something to change the situation, Louie returned to his store front lair on Bath Avenue, and immediately called Little Nick, who said he loved the idea and gave Louie permission to contact Sam Sweets in Chicago, and Harry Hokum in St. Louis. And so within twenty-four hours a "non-profit group, called FOR OUR BOYS, was formed and tens of thousands of handbills were printed and were read to be distributed that asked for donations. Air time was bought in key areas whose locations were determined by a statistical analysis by several professors of economics.

Money came to a box number located in a Brooklyn Post Office, and the operation went forward. Steaks were bought by the hundreds of pounds, vegetables by the bushel; spaghetti, nearly a ton of it, was packed for the trip to Fort Bliss. And there was coffee, wine, and an enormous assortment of pastries including cannoli. This took several days, during which F.K. continued his journey to Washington, and events in Fort Bliss and El Paso continued to happen in their unhistorical but meaningful way.

* * *

It was not quite twilight when the Texas Eagle made one of its several "whistle stops." From the window F.K. saw that the station itself was nothing more than a wooden platform with a series of six steps that led to a parking lot. Surprisingly there were at least five picks-ups that he could see, and people left and boarded the train from the coach cars. Beyond the platform not much more than the parched Texas landscape was visible. It was scrub land, and people who lived on it and worked it were generally as hard and dry-looking as the land.

He turned away from the window just in time to see a woman holding a baby with one arm and a black cardboard valise, and a shopping bag filled with what he guessed were things for the child. She was looking for a seat, and F.K. offered her one next to him, helping her place the shopping bag and the valise next to the field bags of soldiers. He guessed her to be somewhere between twenty and twenty-five years old. She was slim, but her breasts were like half grapefruits and still full of milk, the kind of milk he hadn't tasted in years. She wore a gold wedding ring and a very small diamond engagement ring, a cheap floral patterned dress, anklets and sneakers.

Once she was settled, F.K. introduced himself and his other traveling companions. Her name was Leanna and she was returning to Texarkana where her husband, Captain Troy Visigoth was stationed. She had been visiting her parents.

After the exchange of names, there wasn't much to talk about. Leanna quickly dozed, but managed to hold her baby, Troy junior, tightly to her. Asleep, she had a child-like look about her that made F.K. smile. She wasn't beautiful, but there was something very appealing about her face. It was more rectangular than round or square. A multicolored headband held her dark brown hair away from her face. If he had any facility sketching, he would have sketched her face.

Suddenly, Troy junior became fretful.

She awoke immediately and said, "He needs to be fed."

F.K. expected her to offer the child one of her breasts, but instead of her breast she dug into the shopping bag and pulled out a milk bottle complete with a rubber nipple. "I hope it hasn't spoiled," she said, wrapping a bib around the baby.

"Smell it," F.K. said.

She did and said, "It's gone."

"Give it here," F.K. told her. "I'll get you fresh milk."

"Where?"

"The railroad cow," he said, taking the bottle from her and leaving his seat, he walked out of the car toward the club car and the dining car.

A few minutes later he returned with fresh milk, and a porter holding five opened bottles of beer for his three companions, Leanna and himself. "Got something to drink before dinner," F.K. announced from his place next to Leanna. From her wide eyed look of gratitude, F.K. knew it would be easy to seduce her. She either wasn't very experienced with men, or her hubby was less than gentle with her. But he wasn't even interested in trying, which he knew wasn't like him at all. Seducing a woman required concentration and an acute awareness of the subtle changes in the woman's responses to his words and movements, and he wasn't up to that kind of intensity. His thoughts were elsewhere; namely, on what he would face in Washington and how he would deal with it.

Despite the fact that he and Ramblin' could wind up going to jail for failing to properly answer whatever questions the members of the Committee would ask them, they were determined to "take the high ground" at the very beginning of their interrogation. It was a dangerous maneuver, and if they couldn't achieve it, they would no doubt be turned over to the Federal Authorities and be prosecuted.

Neither he nor Ramblin' wanted to be heroes, but because they were newspaper men, they knew what was at risk. Because F.K. had fought, suffered and killed to keep the country free, he wasn't about to let some "tin horn politicos" cop the country under the guise of protecting it from a real or imagined threat. His thoughts weren't sequential or logical; they drifted in and out of his consciousness. But he was acutely aware of them, even when he was playing poker with his companions. He purposefully lost more hands than he won, and then he dozed until dinner time, at which point he insisted Leanna, junior and the three GIs, accompany him to the dining car.

This time the Maître de did not bother to stop him and his entourage. And everyone ate heartily. F.K. ordered a bottle of red wine and they drank to their having good luck, which certainly the men going to Korea would need to return home unscathed, and he would need if he and Ramblin' would avoid going to jail. As for Leanna, he couldn't even begin to guess what she would or would not need.

By 2100 everyone was more or less asleep. The conductor must have thrown a light blanket over F.K. and Leanna because there was one covering the both of them. And he realized that she'd snuggled against him and that one of his hands was on her right breast, while the other was pressed against his chest. He smiled. But he did not move lest he disturb her. She wore lilac scented perfume, and he found it pleasant to inhale.

"Hold me," she whispered softly.

"What?" he asked, not sure that he heard her correctly.

She repeated what she said, but this time she pressed his hand against her breast.

He could feel the rapid beating of her heart.

She kissed him, pushing her tongue deep into his mouth; and he responded in kind by gently squeezing her breast.

"You want me?" she asked.

Now there was no denying that he did and he answered with a "Yes."

MACKENNA'S PIECE

"My husband doesn't do it often," she said. "When he does, it's quick."

He moved his hand into her crotch; it was wet.

"Not with your fingers," she said. "I want you inside of me."

"Can't do that here."

"Where?"

"An empty roomette," he said.

"What's that?"

"Follow me," he told her.

Together they left their seats and went into the next car. The conductor was there. "An empty roomette," F.K. said, waving two twenties in from him.

"The fourth one," he said, taking the two bills.

"Much obliged," F.K. said.

Within minutes they were naked and humping away on the seat; she came first, howling like an alley cat; then he climaxed with a wolf-like growl. Their coupling was fast and furious. And she stretched out and began playing with his cock and when it was rigid again, she sat on his face giving him her cunt while she mouthed his cock. This time their orgasms were slower in coming, deliberately so. Again she came first, the howling was replaced with soft, explosive "Oh … Oh …Oh!" And then he came with the same primeval grunt of satisfaction.

"I knew it would be good the moment I saw you," she said.

He laughed and repeated the old adage, "You can't tell a book by its cover."

"Maybe you can't, but I can," she said.

167

He smiled. In the distance, down the road two maybe three years he could see her in a divorce court claiming sexual incompatibility. They waited awhile before they had one more go at it. But as far as he was concerned, being seduced by a lovely looking young woman added a fillip to the adventure; for all his sexual encounters, that was the first time it happened, every man's dream, every man's fantasy.

* * *

The hail made marching difficult, if not impossible and very quickly the men took it upon themselves to break step and walk as fast possible, then they began to run. The parade turned into a melee of men trying to get out of "harm's way," of very large hail stones, one of which hit Shanahan on his forehead when he looked up instead of keeping his head down and shielding his face. The blow was so forceful that it knocked him down and required Fragola, whose tent was practically shredded by the onslaught of the hail, to operate out of the back of an ambulance.

When Shannahan was brought to Fragola's attention, he was still groggy from the blow; and Fragola's sense of humor dictated that he tell the Lieutenant not too worry too much because the front part of his brain, the frontal lobe, had separated from the rest it and would in time reconnect. This was related in a combination of Latin and Italian. The Latin was a mishmash of medical terminology and the Italian was recipe for meat balls and spaghetti with Marinara sauce.

The news put Shanahan in such an anxious emotional state that he passed out and had to be revived, and was reassured that he had nothing to worry about, than tens of thousands of people lead perfectly normal lives with half their brains missing.

Still staggered by the enormity of his condition, Shanahan, nodded and said, "I'll try my best."

"You do that," Fragola answered, "and no one will notice any change in you." And just to add a little whipped cream on the cup cake, he put Shanahan on limited duty for the next twenty-four hours.

But Celenza was so badly dehydrated, he had to be rushed to the William Beaumont Army Hospital where the necessary IVs were inserted into both his arms in order to hydrate him and restore his electrolyte balance. There were two dozen men in the same condition and all of them were hospitalized.

When the men of 245th returned to Logan Heights, they were exhausted. They had not only endured the pounding of the hail, which was followed by torrential downpour and then again by the searing heat of the temperature spike.

Major Davidson suggested to Colonel Miller that the men be allowed to rest the following day, but he would have none of that "wussy stuff," adding, "The men have to ready themselves for the maneuvers."

Davidson wasn't satisfied with the Colonel's answer, and wrote an ambiguous memo to the company commanders allowing them to give the men more recreational time than the training schedule called for. He also wrote up a citation for MacKenna, commending him on his quick response to Celenza's "near fatal condition."

Polly and Carmine were too exhausted to work on the 201 files of the new men, and with Second Lieutenant Sedgwick Hardback in command while Celenza was out, neither one felt any degree of urgency. As Polly succinctly stated, "Hardback didn't know his ass from his elbow." But both men couldn't help commenting on MacKenna's rapid response to Celenza's condition.

"It was almost as though he knew it was going to happen," Polly said.

"There's more to that guy, no matter how many degrees he has," Carmine answered. "It's like he's not for real."

Polly leaned back in his chair and considered what Carmine said before he asked, "If he ain't for real, what the hell is he doing here?"

Carmine gave his usual shrug.

"I hear some shit that Mastrangelo told one of the medics that when he drove down to the main base the other day he saw him yakin' with a bird colonel and a general."

"Yeah, like I talk to God," Carmine answered.

Their conversation stopped and each was left his own thoughts about MacKenna.

* * *

When Silvia first heard that Celenza was in the hospital, she became very upset and wept copiously, even before she went to the hospital and saw him decorated with several IVs. She, in the fashion of a true martyr blamed her recent thoughts and actions for Thomas' condition. But when the nurse assured her that he'd back on duty within forty-eight hours, she felt much better and immediately phoned Angie to tell her what had happened.

Rather than to continue their phone conversation and because Angie said that she had something very important to speak to her about, they agreed to meet in an hour at Maria's Coffee Shop, two blocks south of the El Paso Del Norte Hotel.

If weather could have the quality of whimsy, then it might also be said that it was at its most whimsical because the city of El Paso, was bone dry and full heat-producing sunshine. The hail storm hadn't touched the city. But the intense heat made the sidewalks and roadways look wavy.

Both women wore summer frocks and arrived at the coffee shop within a minutes of each other, Angie first, then Silvia. At first the conversation was still about Tom and his heat exhaustion.

"But I was assured he'd be back on duty within forty-eight hours," Silvia said, after each of them gave the Mexican waitress their orders for coffee and blueberry pie with a scoop of chocolate chip mint ice cream.

Angie took the lead in the conversation that followed, explaining that after her confession to Father Soufflé, she had second thoughts about going for instruction.

"Now that's strange," Silvia said, "because I was feeling the same way about Father Dominiche."

"I'm certain I heard him—"

171

"Like he was doing it to himself?"

Angie nodded and said, "And wanted him to do it to me."

"That's what I thought too," Silvia said.

"I did some checking," Angie said. "Father Soufflé has a reputation for—" She stopped speaking when the waitress approached the table with their orders. But as soon as they were alone again, she said, "I'm not going."

"Neither am I," Silvia said resolutely.

"We confessed, that's enough," Angie commented.

"Besides, priests aren't supposed jerk off while hearing a confession or want to fuck the woman who's confessing," Silvia said.

"No way," Angie agreed.

"I mean, what happened happened and it's not going to happen again."

They looked at each other for several moments before Angie asked, "Is it?"

Silvia shrugged.

"What does that mean?"

"I don't know," Silvia said softly. "It was different than when I do it with Tom."

Angie nodded.

Silvia reached across the table and took hold of Angie's left hand, "It's our secret."

"Yes," Angie said.

"We'll just let nature take its course," Silvia responded.

"Yes, that's what we'll do."

"Maybe once in a while, just to celebrate something special."

"Yes," Silvia gently squeezing Angie's hand, then letting go of it.

"But I'm still interested in *ménage à trois*," Angie said.

Both laughed.

* * *

For the remainder of the day, all duty was cancelled with the exception of Guard and mess hall. Most of the men took advantage of the unexpected "holiday" by sleeping, and drinking as much water as they could at any one time.

During this interval, MacKenna requisitioned a jeep and drove to the William Beaumont Army Hospital to visit Celenza to confirm what he had already guessed was the source of F.K.'s information for his articles about nuclear 50 caliber bullets.

Celenza shared a room with six other men, all of whom were victims of heat exhaustion; and like Celenza they had IVs in their arms.

"Thanks," Celenza said when MacKenna came up to his bed.

They shook hands.

"I need to speak to you about a sensitive issue," MacKenna said, pulling up a chair very close to Celenza's bed.

"Trappaso giving you trouble?"

"No. It has nothing to do with him," MacKenna answered.

Celenza raised his eyebrows.

"First, you have to swear not to speak to anyone about our conversation, not even your wife," MacKenna whispered. "Whatever you say or I say is classified information. Do you understand that?"

"Yes," Celenza said with a nod, surprised that a sergeant would speak to him that way.

"To begin with, Lieutenant, my name is John Gault. MacKenna is a fictitious name. I'm a Colonel in the CID."

Celenza's heart skipped a beat; then raced.

"I'm assigned to the Two Forty Fifth to investigate a certain situation that I can not divulge, but then this thing about nuclear fifty caliber ammo came up and I was assigned to find out where that came from, since it cuts very close to something else the army is doing here at Fort Bliss. Have you any questions?" MacKenna asked.

Celenza shook his head.

"When I picked you up and carried you to the Medics, you said a few things that you probably would not have said if you were in a normal state."

Celenza swallowed hard. He was sure that he was in trouble, deep trouble.

"I know that the misinformation about ammo came from you, but I need to know the circumstances, and I especially need to know who you gave the information to."

Celenza opened and closed his fists several times before he said, "My wife and Trappaso's wife, Angie are very good friends. And when I promoted you to section chief, Trappaso told Angie and Angie told my wife, and she called her father who called mine and I made up the story about the ammo to get my dad off my back about why I switched Vinny to S-3.

"How did the information get from her to the reporter?" MacKenna asked.

Celenza shook his head. "I'll be damned if I know."

MacKenna leaned against the back of the chair. "You know I'll have to question your wife?"

"Yes, I know," Celenza sighed.

"I'll see her sometime tomorrow," MacKenna said. "But you have nothing to worry about and neither does she," MacKenna said. "It just happened that the newspaper story cut too close to something else and the Brass got upset."

"She's going to be scared shitless when you show up," Celenza said.

"I know, especially when I tell her I'm from the CID."

"You can bet on it," Celenza answered.

"I'll see you back in the area," MacKenna said. "Remember our conversation is classified; it never took place."

They shook hands and as MacKenna left, Celenza asked, "Do you know what *ménage à trois* is?"

MacKenna wanted to laugh, but he didn't. "A *ménage à trois* is a combination of three people having sex," he said, "usually two women and one man or two men and one woman."

"Holy Christ, how the hell did Silvia—" Celenza stopped and shook his head. "That's some fucking threesome thing."

MacKenna shrugged and said, "Shit happens." And he left, knowing he had half the story; he was sure Silva would provide the other half. But he would have to wait until the next day to get it. He was dog tired and the temperature had cooled down to a mere ninety degrees.

CHAPTER IX

Early the next morning Shanahan received a phone call from Base Intelligence ordering him to report immediately to Colonel Charles Hargrove. Once again Mastrangelo was his driver.

"Base Intelligence," Shanahan said, settling himself on the rear seat. He wasn't going to sit next to the driver the way most of the officers do, and since the driver was Mastrangelo, he was more inclined to ride "piggy back" than less. Besides, he wanted to think about what he was sure would be praise for his report on MacKenna and Davidson, and perhaps his dream of being transferred to the War Department in Washington would be within his reach.

Mastrangelo for his part was happy that Shanahan was behind him. Up front, he was so fuckin' fat, part of him spilled off the seat and practically rested on the shift, making it difficult to move. But more important, he didn't like him; and when he spoke to Sal about him, Sal said, "Only Shanahan likes Shanahan."

The drive took twenty minutes, but Mastrangelo purposefully exceeded the speed limit of forty miles an hour and drove closer to fifty-five miles an hour. They were in a parking slot at the rear of the building before Shanahan realized it. "Wait for me," he said, slowly extricating himself from the rear of the Jeep. It was easier getting in than out. But once out, he straightened up and assumed a military posture with his belly hanging over his belt.

As soon as he told the sergeant at the desk who he was, the sergeant called for an orderly who escorted him to the Colonel's office, where a young WAC picked up the phone, dialed a number then announced, "Second Lieutenant Shanahan is here, Sir." She listened for a moment; then said, "Yes, Sir." Put the phone down in its cradle and said, "Go right in Lieutenant, the Colonel is waiting for you."

Shanahan knocked softly on the Colonel's door.

"Come," a voice growled from the other side of the door.

Shanahan entered the office.

"Close the door after you," the Colonel said in the same growling tone he used a moment before.

Shanahan closed the door, as ordered, and stepped forward to the front of the desk, "Lieutenant Shanahan reporting as ordered, Sir."

The Colonel, a tall, thin man with gray eyes stared at him and said nothing.

Shanahan remained at attention.

The Colonel, who was seated, put the forefinger of his right hand on a packet of papers, and said, "Lieutenant, you're an idiot."

All of Shanahan's dreams plummeted into an abyss; he felt as if he too were falling, going down in flames the way plane does when it has been shot out of the sky. He felt it in the pit of his stomach, and though the room was air-conditioned, he was perspiring profusely.

"I don't have the power to reduce your rank, but if I did I would bust you down to a private. To say that your report is barely intelligible and the assumptions are remarkably stupid, would not do justice to their ineptness."

The Colonel stood. "All of your future reports, no matter what the subject are to be vetted by Major Davidson before they are forwarded to Base Intelligence. Is that clear Lieutenant?"

"Perfectly, sir."

"Dismissed," growled the Colonel.

* * *

Shanahan practically staggered out of the office, and when he reached the jeep, he held on to the rear of it and regurgitated his morning breakfast on to the empty parking spot next to Mastrangelo's jeep.

"Watch where it goes," Mastrangelo cautioned. "I don't want to clean my jeep again."

Shanahan looked at him with baleful eyes.

"So you're havin' a bad day," Mastrangelo said with a smile. "You know it happens."

Shanahan heaved himself into the rear of the jeep. "The son-of-a-bitch never gave me a chance to say a word," he complained.

Mastrangelo shrugged. He guessed 'the son-of-a-bitch' was someone who outranked Shanahan. "Too fuckin' bad," he mumbled under his breath.

"I hear that," Shanahan growled.

"Whata you want me to do? Cry maybe?"

"Listen, Ginzo, I can put you—"

Mastrangelo glanced over his shoulder and smiled, "Sure if you want a bullet in your back, or maybe busted legs."

"Are you threatening me?"

"Naw, just tellin' it to you like it is."

Shanahan said nothing and chewed on his lower lip. He knew that Mastrangelo wasn't just blowing smoke rings. The damn Mafia was all over the place, even in the goddam army. "Go to El Paso. I have to get cleaned up. There's a cafe, Julio's, on the corner of Adobe and Cactus streets. Go there."

"Yeah, I know where it is. Got good coffee and ice cream," Mastrangelo answered, already looking forward to a cup of coffee and a dish of vanilla chocolate chip ice cream.

There was another jeep and a white Chevy parked in front of Julio's when they got there. Shanahan hesitated. If that was brass, he'd have to explain what he was doing there at eleven hundred, and that was the last thing he wanted to do.

"Mastrangelo, check it out," he ordered. "I want to know—"

"If there's brass in there."

"Just fucking do it," Shanahan growled.

Mastrangelo was out of the Jeep and back in less than thirty seconds. "You ain't gonna fuckin' believe it."

The Colonel?"

Mastrangelo shook his head.

"Major Davidson?"

"Sergeant MacKenna and two stunning looking broads: Celenza's and Trappaso's wives."

"Holy Christ!"

"Yeah, that too," Mastrangelo said.

Shanahan suddenly saw an opportunity to redeem himself. He shifted himself out of the Jeep and said to Mastrangelo, "You stay here."

"No way," Mastangelo answered. "I ain't goin' to miss the fun."

Shanahan tried to stare him down, but couldn't. "Okay, come with me; but keep your fucking mouth shut. *Capisce*?"

Mastrangelo nodded and followed Shanahan into Julio's, where MacKenna, Silvia and Angie occupied a booth, and the law of coincidence triumphed, putting several people in the same place; three of whom had a valid reason for being there, one of whom stumbled upon the three; and the fourth, Mastrangelo was there out of happenstance.

Shanahan strode boldly up to the booth where MacKenna and the two ladies were sitting and bellowed, "Sergeant, just what exactly do you think you're doing?"

"Having a conversation with these two women," MacKenna answered. He saw Shanahan and Mastrangelo when they first pulled up in front of the cafe and was sure that Shanahan wouldn't miss the opportunity to exercise his authority.

"Why aren't you with your section?"

"Because, I'm here Lieutenant. No one can be in two places at the same time."

"Don't wise mouth me," Shanahan shouted, his face flushing.

"Stop shouting, Lieutenant, you're embarrassing me and my guests, besides annoying the other people here."

"What?"

"You heard me," MacKenna said. "Now, I'd appreciate if you let me get on with my reason for being here."

"Mastrangelo you're my witness," Shanahan said.

"I didn't see or hear nothing," Mastrangelo answered.

Shanahan's face turned a deeper red.

"Lieutenant, come with me into the men's room," MacKenna said, "I have something to show you."

"What?"

"Shanahan, for once don't be a horse's ass," MacKenna said, his tone unlike the one he spoke a few moments before." And after he excused himself from Silvia and Angie, he slid out of the booth and headed for the men's room with Shanahan in tow. Inside, he made sure that no one else was there before he said, "I'm Colonel John Gault, CID." And he showed Shanahan his ID. "What I'm doing is none of your business. Have your coffee and leave. And if I discover that you revealed my identity to anyone, you'll be on the next plane to Korea. Do you understand?"

"Oh my God!" Shanahan wailed.

"He's out of the picture; this is between the two of us. Keep your mouth shut," MacKenna said. "Now pull yourself together. Your face needs a good washing with cold water. I'm going back to my guests. Have coffee and whatever else you might want and tell the waiter or counter man to put it on my bill. That goes for Mastrangelo as well."

Shanahan nodded.

"Do I hear a 'Yes, Sir?'"

"Yes, Sir," Shanahan said.

MacKenna nodded, and with a smile, left the men's room.

* * *

There are two parts to this section of the story. The first part concerns MacKenna, Silvia and Angie and how they happened to be in Julio's in the first place. The answer is simple: MacKenna phoned Silvia, told her that Tom asked him to meet her, which was a lie; and Silvia phoned Angie and asked her to come with her to meet someone who was important. Angie agreed and both were disappointed when they saw MacKenna's Sergeant's stripes. They thought that maybe he'd be at least a Major.

Their introductions were nearly over when Shanahan arrived, but now he and Mastrangelo were safely on the far side of Julio's and MacKenna was back on the seat facing the two women explain that the reason why he wanted to meet with Silvia was to confirm this theory about what had happened.

Before he got down to the nitty gritty of his inquiry, he summoned the waiter and asked the ladies to order whatever they had a taste for. For a few moments both ladies seemed reluctant to act, but MacKenna smiled at them and said, "Please, anything. You're my guests."

His smile and the softness of his words convinced them and both ordered the same thing: three scoops of ice cream—Pistachio, Mint Chocolate, and Butter Pecan topped with generous whipped cream and a dash of cherry brandy. MacKenna's order was more

Spartan: black coffee and a scoop of Vanilla ice-cream.

While they waited for their orders, MacKenna explained that he was the one who'd replaced Vinny as Section Chief of the Heavy Weapons Section, and he apologized to Angie for disrupting their lives. "But it had to be done, said MacKenna. It was Vinny's section or some other section, but the opening happened to be in the Heavy Weapons Section." He skipped over the part that dealt with the feud between Celenza and Gibbs.

MacKenna established an intimacy with the two women by the time their orders were brought to the table. He explained that he was assigned to the 245th for reasons he could not reveal, but he assured them it had nothing to with nuclear ammunition, and he turned his attention to Silvia and said, "Tom already told me the circumstances of how that idea came about."

Silvia tittered. "He told his dad, and I thought it was for real because he told me to forget what I heard."

"Then you called Angie, and told her," MacKenna said.

"We didn't know that the man in the next both—"

"F.K. Pulp."

Both women nodded.

"He was a reporter and heard very word I said," Silvia explained between spoonfuls of ice cream.

"He even picked up our tab, and sent another round of drinks to our table," Angie said. "But we didn't know who he was until a few days later when we went back and he introduced himself."

"And just happened to offer you the opportunity to experience *ménage à trois*," MacKenna said.

Both ladies blushed.

"But nothing happened," Angie offered. "He had to leave."

MacKenna shook his head, "F.K. never passes up a possible opportunity."

"We never heard of it before," Silvia said.

"It's something people do," MacKenna said, realizing the two women in front of him led very sheltered lives in Brooklyn and each on their own was eager to experience something more than their Church's acceptance of the missionary position and perhaps the man on top and the woman underneath. Though a question, as Socrates put it, is the first step toward knowledge, the answer to the question can either be a gift of enlightenment or a gift of misery and frustration.

"We tried to figure it out with stick figures on paper but gave up," Silvia admitted.

Suddenly Angie said, "You could show us, couldn't you?"

The offer took MacKenna by surprise, and he glanced toward Shanahan and Mastrangelo who were still at the counter and wondered what they would think if they had the slightest inkling of what he'd just been offered.

"Thank you—for your trust," MacKenna answered. "But I am here with you on official business and to mix it with personal pleasure would be taking advantage of my—"

"Some other time then," Silvia said. "After maneuvers, maybe."

"No ladies. I'm committed," he said; and suddenly he thought about Flo. She seemed to be the kind of woman whom he could be committed to, who he could fall in love with and maybe marry.

"Oh, we're committed too," Silvia said, "but we're asking you to be our teacher, nothing else."

"Again, I thank you," MacKenna said, adding, "I suggest you finish your ice cream before it melts."

MacKenna's coffee was strong, almost to the point of being bitter, the way he liked it. And there was enough of a pause in his conversation with the two women across the table from him for him to wonder what questions Celenza would ask Silvia when he returned home. Perhaps none. Perhaps he wouldn't want to risk rocking the boat, or perhaps his questions would be directed inwards—where have I failed? What have I done that caused her to wander; though he was almost certain Celenza wouldn't go that way. And he found himself wondering which way he would have gone if a similar situation had arisen in his marriage. He didn't have a ready answer, other than to realize that questions eventually lead to answers, even if the answers are temporary and eventually prove to be false like the giddy feeling that Silvia and Angie would experience with F.K., and the weight of the awful guilt that would follow.

His brow must have furrowed because suddenly Silvia asked, "Is anything wrong?"

"Nothing," MacKenna answered quickly, "just thinking about stuff that has to be done before we go on maneuvers."

"I hope we cleared things up for you," Angie said.

"Yes, you did," he chuckled.

"Is there any chance of our meeting you again?" Silvia questioned.

"Not unless we accidentally bump into each other."

She nodded, looked at her watch and reminded Angie that should be going because their "kids would be home from school soon."

MacKenna stood up, and shaking their hands, he thanked them for their cooperation. When they left, he remained in the booth to organize his thoughts and pay the check. The part of it that resulted from Shanahan and Mastrangelo was significantly larger than the amount that he, Silvia, and Angie racked up.

* * *

Neither Mastrangelo nor Shanahan spoke to each other while they were at Julio's or in the Jeep on the way back to Logan Heights. But each of them were very much aware of what had happened: Shanahan because he considered himself a victim, and Mastrangelo because he guessed that whatever went on between MacKenna and Shanahan during their brief visit to the men's room was enough to "scare the shit" out of Shanahan. And as far as he was concerned that was okay with him. Later he'd tell Sal about it and find out what he thought happened. One thing he was sure of was that they weren't playing patty cake.

They were almost at Logan Heights when Shanahan smacked his forehead. The truth struck him the way a bolt of lightning blasts a tree: he had fingered the wrong people. Celenza was "the chigger in the woodpile." He was the communist; it stood to reason. After all he was a wop, a ginzo and "you can't trust them as far as you can throw them." Now that he knew MacKenna was CID and was questioning Celenza's and Trappaso's wives, it all made sense. Now, he'd have to "keep a sharp eye" on Celenza when he rejoined the unit.

With the problem finally solved, he faced another one: who would believe him. The only other person who knew what Celenza was up to was MacKenna, and he knew that MacKenna wouldn't touch him with a ten foot pole. But he couldn't let a Commie get away with giving secret information to the Russians.

Charged with the idea that he finally found the true culprit, he entered Headquarters with the demeanor of a man with an important mission only to be pounced on by Gibbs, who, despite their differences in rank, shouted, "Where the fuck have you been? The Colonel has been yelling his head off for you."

Shanahan blanched, deflated and said, "I was—"

"I don't give a flying fuck where you were. Get your ass to the Colonel now or you won't have an ass to go anywhere with."

Gibbs verbal assault caused much laughter, and it was Semelinsky's laughter that Shanahan resented the most.

* * *

As soon as Shanahan entered the Colonel's office, the Colonel was on his feet; and red faced with anger, he roared, "Not five minutes ago I got a call from Brigade about a certain report, and five minutes before that they got a call from Base Intelligence about a certain report that you happened to be the author of. Explain."

Shanahan's innards felt like the wave he once saw in a Japanese painting. His second breakfast was rapidly working its way up.

"Just don't stand there... I want to know why—" The Colonel never finished his sentence because that wave churning inside Shanahan's guts gave his face a sickly green color and he spewed undigested bacon and eggs, coffee and toast on to the top of Colonel Miller's desk, making his copy of The Daily Racing Form unreadable.

"My God you just vomited on my desk," he shouted, astonished that such outrage could occur.

"Colonel, I—" Shanahan began, but was quickly halted by a second wave consisting of cherry-vanilla ice cream and more coffee.

The Colonel rushed to the door and yelled, "Gibbs, in here on the double."

Instantly Gibbs obeyed, and when he saw and smelled the mess that Shanahan created he looked at the Colonel and asked, "The hospital or Doc Fragola?"

"Please, not the hospital," Shanahan managed to say.

"Fragola, then," the Colonel said.

Gibbs opened the door, "Sergeant Kubel get Doc Fragola and a medic here on the double."

Miller looked at Shanahan, who was heaving enormous sighs of grief coupled with tears streaming from his eyes and shook his head. "I have no choice but to tell you that you are no longer the two forty fifth's Intelligence Officer."

Shanahan bawled even louder than before.

"As soon as you're able to, you will report to Captain Verhey and assist him in any way that he needs to be assisted. But as a warning, stay out of his way."

Shanahan wiped the spittle and tears off his face with a dirty handkerchief, but suddenly realizing the reality of the abyss he had just been dropped into, he wept even more knowing that no one cared what happened to him.

Disgusted by the way Shanahan was acting doomed, he said, "Shanahan get a hold of yourself; you're in the fucking army, not a girl's school. Act like a man, even if you aren't one."

Fragola and Sal popped into the office. Fragola's violin practice had been interrupted and he was in a foul mood. One look at Miller's desk gave him a good idea of what happened but not why. But Sal, because Mastrangelo told him about Shanahan's and MacKenna's quick trip to the men's room in Julio's ice cream parlor and its effect of Shanahan, knew that what he was looking at was somehow connected to Mastrangelo's story.

"He wrote a report indicating that Major Davidson and MacKenna were communist agents and handed it into Base Intelligence without showing it to me," Miller said, adding that he had gotten a phone call from Sides "that really burned my ass."

"Shanahan you're an idiot," Fragola said.

Sal guffawed.

Fragola shot him a quick look of reprimand, and said, "That wasn't meant to be funny."

"Sir, but it was; it was your tone," Sal answered.

Fragola waved Sal's answer away; and speaking to Miller, he said, "I'll give him a couple of shots: one to take care of his stomach, and the other to make him sleep. By tomorrow morning he'll be the old Shanahan."

"A shot to make him a new Shanahan," Gibbs said, "would be more in order."

"Sadly, no can do," Fragola said, digging in his black bag for a syringe.

Shanahan took one look at the needle and his knees buckled.

Sal caught him just before he fell, and wrestled him on to a chair. "He's no fuckin' light weight," he commented, stepping back from him.

Fragola gave Shanahan the two shots, and said, "There lays our Caesar. He's going to need help getting back to the BQ. And you're going to have to get that mess off your desk, or you'll have every fly in Texas on it in short order."

* * *

Before MacKenna returned the Jeep to the Motor Pool, he stopped at the Dairy Queen to phone Flo to ask her to have dinner with him as soon as the maneuvers were over.

"And that's all you want to have?" she asked.

"We'll discuss any other arrangements when we're together."

"I always like to know in advance when someone expects to get into me," she said.

"That's fair enough," MacKenna answered.

"Well?"

"With an invitation like that, I'd be a fool not to accept it," he said.

They laughed and simultaneously said, "See you soon."

MacKenna clicked off, paused for a few moments in the phone booth to remember what she looked like naked, smiled and then left to drive back to the 245th area.

* * *

Word of Shanahan's "fall from grace" spread quickly through the battalion, and no one was unhappy about it. And that afternoon the Colonel and Major Davidson discussed the situation. Getting Shanahan out of S-2 created a problem; there wasn't anyone to take his place. All of the officers held specific assignments. Both men knew that to go into the field for five days of maneuvers without an Intelligence Officer would be foolhardy, and probably be scored against them by the officers assigned to rate their performance.

Davidson thought about suggesting MacKenna as a temporary replacement, but instead he opted to wait for the Colonel to take the initiative, which he did by summoning Gibbs and laying out the problem for him.

Gibbs puffed manfully on his pipe while listening to Miller, and when he was finished, Gibbs instantly saw the way to snooker Celenza; but, subtle in his ways, he wrinkled his brow and said nothing.

"Well," Miller said impatiently, "What's your fucking answer?"

Gibbs rubbed his chin, puffed on his pipe a few times before he said, "MacKenna."

Major Davidson wanted to laugh, but instead he coughed a few times and apologized by saying, "A bit of something got caught in my windpipe."

"MacKenna!" Miller exclaimed, as if the name was brand new to him.

"He's got all the qualifications," Davidson said.

Miller looked confused and said, "That's the guy that Celenza—"

"The same one," Gibbs said.

"It would only be on a temporary basis," Davidson said.

"What's his rank?"

"That's debatable."

"What does that mean?"

"According to Celenza's orders, he's a Tech Sergeant, but only acting because he hasn't stood before the reviewing board yet," Gibbs said.

"Then he's really a Private First Class."

"Just a private; he's one of the draftees."

Miller made a humming sound; then he asked Davidson what his take on the situation was.

"Well," Davidson began slowly, "the orders to relieve Shanahan of his S-2 assignment haven't been cut yet, so he can still sign off as the S-2 Officer on anything that comes a across the desk, but MacKenna could occupy the desk; then after the maneuvers are over we can sort things out."

Thinking Davidson was on his side with where MacKenna belonged, Gibbs smiled and said, "We could live with that."

"During the time that we're in the field, MacKenna will wear two hats: Section Chief of A Company's Heavy Weapons Section and Intelligence Sergeant," Davidson said.

Splitting MacKenna that way wasn't what Gibbs had hoped for; it was a Solomon-like decision, but he had to accept it.

"What about his clearances?" the Colonel asked.

"You wouldn't believe what he's cleared for," Davidson said.

"Well then, that's one problem out of the way," Miller announced, glancing at his watch; it was almost three o'clock, time to call his bookie.

* * *

When MacKenna was informed of his new role by Carmine, who got the information over the phone from Gibbs, he accepted it with a shrug.

"Celenza is going to be real pissed when he's told," Polly offered. He was at his desk listening to the conversation between the 1st and MacKenna.

"Don't matter whether he is or he isn't," Carmine answered, "that's the way it's gonna be."

Again MacKenna shrugged. He was feeling pretty good; he'd solved one problem and the other one would shortly be solved. But now he needed the use of typewriter for an hour or to write his report to Base Intelligence and asked Polly if he could use his.

"Help yourself," Polly answered vacating the chair at his desk. If Carmine was there, this would be the opportunity to speak to MacKenna; and then, as if Carmine could read his thoughts, he said, "I'm going to check out a couple things."

"Listen MacKenna," Polly said, as soon as he and MacKenna were alone, "I'm not going to beat around the bush. You saved me a beating, maybe even saved my life, so I owe you."

MacKenna knew what was coming.

"Gibbs and I run a two for five operation," Polly said. "And I want you to be part of it."

"I'm listening," MacKenna said.

"See, I have dreams. I want to buy into Manelo's. He's got a good business going. But it could be expanded and made really classy."

"With gambling?"

"Absolutely," Polly responded. "Pussy, drinking and gambling are a perfect trio."

"What about Gibbs? I mean, what does he think about me joining the two of you?"

"He has reservations."

"So do I," MacKenna said.

"Shoot."

"What would be my cut?"

"A third."

"On Manelo's as well?"

Polly nodded.

"So far so good," MacKenna said.

"Then it's a deal," Polly said, offering his hand.

"Not quite. I want the book," MacKenna told him though he wasn't sure whether Polly or Gibbs had it. But it seemed more likely that it was in Polly's possession; since he made the contacts and handed out the money.

Polly withdrew his hand. "No can do. Gibbs would blow his stack."

"No book, no deal," MacKenna said, beginning to type.

Polly knew better than to argue with MacKenna, and he said, "Hold the fort. I'll be back in few minutes."

"Will do," MacKenna answered, knowing he was going to arrange a meeting with Gibbs.

* * *

F.K.'s train was side-tracked to allow a troop train filled with black troops to pass. By the time it reached Texarkana, it was an hour and half late. Preparing to detrain, Leanna gathered up her baby and her small cardboard suitcase.

F.K. was sorry to see her go; she gave delicious head and she herself had lovely taste and scent. Always the gentleman, he offered to see her off the train.

She shook her head. "My husband is a very jealous man," she said. "He'd really give me a rough time if he saw us together."

"Understood," F.K. said, silently admitting that if he were in the husband's place he'd be jealous too. The Green Eyed Monster has a way of getting to men, especially if a woman is involved who they deem is their property. He gave her a quick kiss on her forehead and an equally quick hug before they said goodbye, and he returned to his seat in a pensive mood.

He wasn't proud of his philandering, and knew that it made his wife unhappy as it would any wife who loved her husband. He knew all of the psychological palaver that tries to explain why certain men are always on the hunt for pussy, and he didn't believe any of it. He wasn't out to prove himself or anything else... That was his last thought before he dozed.

* * *

Celenza was released from the William Beaumont Army Hospital at eighteen hundred hours and rode the bus into El Paso and another one for a short distance to where he lived. During the thirty hours he'd spent in the hospital, he had time to think about his marriage, especially after MacKenna told him what *ménage à trois* meant. That Silvia might have been involved in *ménage à trois* enraged him at first. Despite his hypochondria and his worrisome nature, he was still a man and coveted his wife. But after a couple of hours, his anger dissipated, dissolved in its own heat, leaving in its wake the grief of a cuckold. But that too passed because "if push came to shove" he would have to "own up" to having had extra-marital encounters, a couple with Angie.

It was on the bus ride from the hospital to El Paso that he realized he loved Silvia and didn't want to end his marriage to her, that in a few months he'd be in Korea fighting for his life; and if he was lucky enough to "come home," he want to come home to her and his kids. He also realized that there was nothing spectacular about him, that eventually he'd own his father's paint store. That wasn't a glamorous future, but it would provide a good income and enable them to live without financial worry.

By the time he arrived home, he was happy to be there and Silvia greeted him with hugs and kisses, so did his children. Sometime later he would speak to her about how she came to know about *ménage à trois*. But now he would accept the fact she'd learned about it by doing it, the way he accepted the fact that she'd "lost her virginity" by horseback riding, something he found out was impossible a few years after they were married, not that it would have stopped him from marrying her. He was in love with her then, and he still loved her . . .

* * *

Polly and Gibbs met in their usual place, but they didn't stay there. They boarded the bus for El Paso, and went to small bar, not far from the Alligator Park. Settled in a booth, they ordered Tex-Mex Chili, the cook's specialty, and two beers.

There wasn't much conversation between them, except for a few comments on the coming maneuvers where Gibbs had said that they were "unprepared for any field exercises," and Polly, who was a novice at the game of being a soldier said that he didn't think much about it because he had "other things on his mind."

They ate in silence, finished their beers and ordered two more before Gibbs said. "Okay, let's talk."

"MacKenna wants in," Polly said.

Gibbs didn't answer immediately. In a way that he couldn't define, MacKenna spooked him. There was something about the man that didn't "sit right" with him. The more he thought it, the more he felt that in some mysterious way MacKenna was playing all of them as if they were puppets. "What's the deal?" he finally asked.

"He'll supply more cash, enough to buy into Manelo's."

"His cut."

"A third of everything."

Gibbs put his palms against the table's edge and pushed hard on it moving himself against the side of the booth. "And what did you say," Gibbs questioned.

"I'd speak to you."

"Okay, you spoke to me," Gibbs said.

"So, what's your answer?"

"I don't trust him; there's something that doesn't add up."

"He's willing to invest—"

"Just a third of the take and nothing else?"

"The book."

"Are you crazy?"

"He wants to keep the record—"

"Absolutely not," Gibbs said, pushing ever harder against the table. "Good God, where the fuck is your brain? If he has the book, he has us."

"Not if he's part of the operation," Polly countered.

"I don't trust him."

"Why?"

"I don't know 'why.' I just don't, period. Besides, I don't have to give you a reason."

"In this case you do," Polly said. He was angry. Gibbs was being unreasonable.

"Listen and listen good," Gibbs said, "he's got too many fuckin' degrees. He knows too much about too many things, and he can speak and understand too many fuckin' languages."

"Those are piss poor reasons not to trust him."

"They're my fuckin' reasons, understand?"

"No, I don't understand."

Gibbs removed his hands from the edge of the table and placed his elbows on it and locked his hands. "I'm against it."

"I'm for it," Polly said.

"Where does that leave us?"

"I'll do it alone if you don't want to be part of it."

"You see the dollars and you go for it."

"I see a chance to make money, and I want to go for it."

"Then you go for it," Gibbs said, dropping a ten dollar bill on the table. "That'll cover my share and the tip. I'm out of here."

Polly took several deep breaths before he called for his check. There was no doubt in his mind that

Gibbs was "a stupid son-of-a-bitch." He would give the book to MacKenna after the maneuvers.

* * *

Leo the Tiger's boss pulled all sorts of strings: congressmen, a few senators, a couple of generals and before he was finished, he had twenty duce and half ton trucks, and ten three quarter ton vehicles and ten jeeps, all with drivers, at his disposal, which meant that Leo the Tiger had the necessary wheels to deliver the food to the 245th Infantry Battalion.

In addition to the donations of food, money came in small and large quantities. The largest sums were donated from organizations and companies where Leo and others like him had connections. It turned out to be a very lucrative operation.

Leo the Tiger and three of his body guards rode in the leading jeep. Behind him, in the other jeeps were the men who would cook and serve the food carried in the duce and half trucks and the three quarter ton jobs. There was more than enough food to feed the battalion for at least two weeks.

Leo's boss also managed to procure three large tents, tables and chairs. The trucks carrying them would join the food convoy a day before it reached Fort Bliss.

Everything was set up to have the FEED THE TROOPS operation run smoothly, but then Leo the Tiger received a phone call from Silvia's father telling him that the 245th was headed for two weeks of maneuvers, somewhere in the desert.

"The desert?"

"That's what my daughter told me."

"I didn't know we got deserts," Leo said.

"I didn't know 'til she told me."

"Don't worry, we will fuckin' find them," Leo said.

"Once you tell me that, Leo, I don't worry."

"Good," Leo said and put the phone down. He leaned back in his chair, cut a cigar and began to smoke it. For a few minutes he sat very still, directing clouds of bluish-white smoke toward the ceiling. The suddenly he bolted up and yelled, "Who the fuck put deserts in Texas?"

None of his boys, who were either busy studying the racing forms, or on the bank of phones on the other side of the taking bets, expected his sudden eruption and immediately stopped whatever they were doing.

"I ask you guys a question and all I get for an answer is a dumb look on all of your ugly faces."

"Boss, you ask a question like that, an' you raise your fist at God," one of the men said.

Leo was a great believer in God and dutifully went to mass every Sunday with his wife and kids. But he seldom went to confession; and when he did, he had to omit telling the priest some of the things he did because he was afraid that the old man would have heart attack in the confessional booth, and he didn't want that on his conscience.

"To the Devil," Leo said, crossing himself. "I raise my fist to the devil"

"Call Vito's son Mark," another man said. "He's in the War Department."

"Good idea," Leo said, "helped get one of our friends a big contract." He took another couple of puffs on the cigar, set it on the rim of blue-glass ash tray and picked up the phone and dialed Mark's number.

CHAPTER X

General Lewis, aka General Loose Cannon had been celebrating his new command with huge dinners, huge catered affairs with subordinates and local people deemed important enough for his social secretary to have invited them. All this time he didn't so as much as glance at the papers on his desk because he was too hung over to understand them. But on Friday afternoon he was sufficiently sober to grasp two pieces of information: the 245th Infantry Battalion was going on field maneuvers for a week in the desert, and that somehow a newspaper reporter F.K. Pulp wrote a story about nuclear .50 caliber ammo that cut close to the experiments that were being carried on at a secret location on the base.

That an infantry unit was in his domain half amused and half angered him. He turned to his aide. "What is the infantry unit supposed to do?"

"Defend a vital road link and railhead from falling into enemy hands, the invading force."

Loose Cannon held up his right hand, signaling that he didn't want to hear any more, and that he was about to speak. "Put the 245th here in the mountains; let them defend this pass, the Cunt. We have some elements of the 82nd with us."

"Yes, Sir."

"Okay, they'll be the attacking force. Don't tell the 245th who the attacking forces is; and we'll see what kind of soldiers those New York boys are. Send the revised orders by teletype. I want both units in the field by Sunday. Scoring will begin Sunday night."

Satisfied that he had taken care of the first issue, he now turned to F.K. Pulp. "I want him here in my office pronto," Loose Cannon declared.

"He's on his way to Washington to answer a subpoena from HUAC," his aide said.

"Good, they'll burn his ass good and proper."

The Aide made no comment.

"Is there anything else that needs my immediate attention," Loose Cannon asked.

"There's some sort of food convoy heading this way."

"Food convoy?

"Yes, Sir. Organized, as I understand it, by prominent members of the New York Mafia."

"You're fucking joking."

"No, Sir, I'm not. According to the information I have they should be entering Texas sometime today."

"Why?"

"The 245th has been on half rations. '

Loose Cannon's ire was up and he strode around the room, using his swagger stick to whack anything that he happened to catch sight of, which was why his aide stayed slightly behind him. "The fucking army travels and fights on its stomach. Napoleon said that a couple of hundred years ago; and it's still true." He stopped. "Where the fuck are you?"

"Here," his aide announced, stepping out from behind Loose Cannon when he was sure the General's swagger stick was tucked under his arm.

"Can you explain why the 245th doesn't have enough rations to feed its men?"

"The Commissary has them down for six hundred rations, but they picked up another four hundred from the rail head. All RA boys. But they've been assigned to the 245th.

"So, as a result of a fuck up somewhere, I have to deal with a Mafia food convoy from New York?"

"That's the big picture."

"Shit, is all I can say," Loose Cannon said, followed by, "I need a drink to settle my stomach and kill he headache that's beginning to play roller ball in my head." He went to his desk, opened the bottom draw and pulled out a bottle of Glenlivet followed by a shot glass and poured himself a drink. "The problem, he said, "is that there are too many goddamn problems"

"Yes, Sir," his aide said.

* * *

Gibbs was in a fury; not only over Polly's desertion, but also MacKenna's sudden appointment to the position of Intelligence Sergeant; and just to scramble matters into an administrative nightmare, Base Headquarters changed the area of maneuvers from the desert to the mountains. No one in Battalion was prepared for that switch.

Major Connelly, the Battalion Ops officer, attempted to appeal the change through Colonel Miller, who wasn't about "to buck the powers that be" for fear of aggravating Brigade.

The change necessitated Sergeant Katz to recalibrate Ops evaluations, statistical and otherwise, which made him almost maniacal, screaming contradictory orders at his clerk typists.

The Cunt, aka known as hill 6969 on the topographical maps, was three thousand feet up, a half a mile long and something like 50 feet wide at its widest point, otherwise its width varied from ten to 30 feet. The pass resulted from a geological uplift of an ancient sea bed sixty to sixty-five million years ago. The two sections of rock on either side of it were smooth and rounded like a human backside. In the imagination of some male topographer, the combination of the smooth rock face and the narrowness of the opening reminded him of a woman's pudenda.

The Colonel, all the Company Commanders and Majors Davidson and Connelly, spent the morning in conference in an effort to devise some sort of reasonable defense plan. The invaders were still expected to come from the south. Neither Brigade nor they were informed that their opposition would consist of two companies from the 82nd Airborne, which would be more than enough to "make mince-meat" out of those wise-guy New Yorkers according to General Loose Cannon.

The defense plan that evolved put Companies A & B on a semicircular half-mile in front of the pass. Company C and most of Company D would provide cover for Headquarters Battery located at the widest section of the pass. And that the part of D Company not assigned to cover Headquarters would cover the back end of the pass that led to an outcropping of rock overlooking the White Sands Testing Area, some twenty five miles away in New Mexico.

After the meeting was adjourned, Davidson showed MacKenna the plan, who nodded and said, "Nothing on top."

"Nothing," Davidson said.

"We can be hit and hit hard," MacKenna commented.

"Yes, we can and probably will be," Davidson answered.

"Connelly know that?"

"Blindsided by his brilliant Operations Sergeant," Davidson said.

MacKenna nodded. "Shit happens."

"It sure does," Davidson answered. "It sure as hell does."

* * *

The more Gibbs thought about Polly's disaffection, the more he realized "the little shit" had him by his balls. There wasn't anyone he could turn to for advice or help without revealing their shylocking enterprise. But there was no doubt in his mind that Polly was a traitor, a poor excuse for a man, as he defined what a man should be according to what he was. As Battalion Sergeant Major he commanded a lot or power, even more than the usual battalion Sergeant Major because of his friendship with Miller. But that friendship wasn't the kind that he would be able to turn to in the circumstance in which he found himself. Polly's willingness to give away a third of their business to MacKenna struck him as being extremely foolish, and compounded to this was the matter of the "book." The "book" was equivalent to the Bible; they lived by it. The book was a roster of who owed what. It held the evidence of their activities.

Gibbs was so irate that the puffs of smoke coming from his pipe came so fast that they quickly became a column that reached to the ceiling and then spread out, covering that part of it that was over him.

As far as he was concerned, Polly needed a lesson or two and needed to be cut down to size, not that there was much to cut down. He was short enough as it was. But with all his pent up anger, Gibbs was stumped. Short of killing him, he couldn't come up with a solution. He thought about setting him up for Philip Trees, but he knew he couldn't trust Philip either.

Without warning, it suddenly came to him. The jar of the recognition was so acute that it forced him to stop puffing on his pipe and leave his chair for a position at the window behind his desk from which he could see the wide expanse of the Battalion Parade Ground and the activity associated with the coming maneuvers. "If you can't fucking beat them, join them," he muttered.

* * *

By Saturday afternoon most of the Battalion trucks were loaded with the necessary supplies, and the men were issued their weapons and the rubber bullets that would be used during the exercise. The departure time from the Battalion area was set for

02:00, with an expected 09:00 arrival times at the Cunt. Those were the times generated by Ops Sergeant Katz, but no one expected them to be "written in stone." In such an operation fuck-ups were expected; and if there weren't any, that in itself would be considered a fuck up because everything clicked, and that, every soldier knows, seldom if ever happens.

Exactly at 19:00 hours, Base Headquarters requested three Duce and halves, drivers and four armed guards with regulation ammo issue to rendezvous at 20:30 with a train at the rail head and station themselves between cars four and six. No other instructions were given. But three trucks had to be unloaded, the men who would be the armed guards appointed and issued clips of live rounds and a Sergeant appointed to lead the small, armed caravan. Davidson requested MacKenna, and Miller approved the request.

MacKenna picked Mastrangelo as his driver. His Duce and half led the two, and only when he saw Doc Fragola and three medics, among them Sal O'Mari, did he realize that detail had something to do with a medical problem.

When they reached the rail head, there were a dozen ambulances from William Beaumont Army Hospital, trucks from other units and many MPs. The train arrived, slowing down before it actually reached the platform at the rail head. It was eighteen cars long, not counting the engine.

Doc Fragola reached their destination before they and he motioned MacKenna to join him.

"Listen, we're taking twenty or so walking wounded to the William Beaumont Psychiatric

Building. They will not be tethered, but if anyone of them breaks away you are to have your men shoot him in his legs. They must not be allowed to get away. They may or not be dangerous."

"Psycho cases?" MacKenna questioned.

Fragola nodded. "I'm here to give each a shot of Thorazine but it might not take effect as quickly as— well, let's hope we don't have to use force."

MacKenna remained silent. The detail was cutting close to his past. When he was finally liberated from a Gestapo Interrogation Center, he was a psycho case. In addition to having his face reconstructed, he needed to have the psychological trauma he suffered sufficiently fixed so that he could get on with his life. He was one of the lucky ones who were able to cross the divide from a psychotic individual to a "normal" one. There were all too many who couldn't make the crossing and remained in military hospitals.

Fragola guessed the MacKenna had once been in a similar condition to the men they were about to load into the trucks and said, "You'll be okay. '

MacKenna thanked him and returned to his truck.

Suddenly the entire rail head was illuminated with huge spot lights, the kind that were used to anti-aircraft units during World War Two to spot enemy planes.

MacKenna assigned armed guards to the doors of cars four and six, repeating the orders he'd been given by Fragola.

After a few minutes the doors of cars four and six opened and what came out of them was a column of men looking more dead than alive. Some were drooling, others were crying. Many laughed hysterically, while a few were absolutely silent. The guard herded them into the rear of the trucks. Several couldn't make it up on to the trucks without help. And a few pissed as they clambered up truck bed.

MacKenna handled them gently; some he touched, others he spoke softly to; and now and then he laughed or smiled.

When all of them were loaded without incident, Fragola signaled MacKenna to begin to drive. They reached the hospital without incident, but when they began to unload the men, several became balky and had to be manhandled by the hospital staff in order to get them into the building.

After the last man was safely in the building, MacKenna thanked the men who were with him and headed back to the Battalion Area on Logan Heights. But none of the men spoke; their collective silence was indicative of their fears. In the months ahead, they too would face the enemy and perhaps they had just seen the fate that awaited them. It was a weight that each one of them would carry until they were safely home, away from the war.

Fargola arrived in the Battalion Area before MacKenna and his detail. And again he signaled MacKenna to join him.

"This is for your guys," he said, handing him two bottles of scotch. "Two shots each," he added.

"Thanks," MacKenna responded.

"Anything that's left over get rid of," Fragola said.

"Yes, Sir," MacKenna said, saluting him.

Fragolar returned the salute. "You're an okay guy, an okay guy."

* * *

MacKenna gave each of his men two shots, and he took two for himself before pouring out what was left, then he went off on his own, but not back to his bunk. He needed to be alone; at least that was what he originally thought. He needed someplace quiet, where he could look back at himself, the person he was and the person he became. Quite suddenly he thought about his dead wife, Karin. She was so young, so beautiful. She never had time to realize how much she contributed to his stability. He needed her again. But that need would have to be satisfied elsewhere, and he crossed Dyer Street to the Queen Bee, where the telephone booth was and dialed Flo's number.

She answered on the first ring. "I was just thinking about you," she told him before he said anything beyond identifying himself.

"That's why I called," he said flippantly. "A bad case of mental telepathy."

"Are you okay?"

"I'm fine."

"I suddenly find myself worrying about you," she said.

"That's nice of you to say that," he responded.

"No," she said. "It means that—"

"I know what it means because I'm having the same reaction and the same feelings. After I wrap things up here, I have some leave time coming. We could spend it together."

"What do mean by 'wrap things up?'" She asked.

"I meant after maneuvers," he said, realizing he let something slip out that he shouldn't have. "I'll be in the field about a week; then, I'll apply for a leave. I have a good deal of time coming to me."

"Where would you like to go?" she asked.

"Anywhere you want to go."

"We'll discuss it," she said.

"Okay," he said.

"Take care of yourself."

"I will," he said, "and you do the same. Take care of yourself." And he clicked off. For several moments he didn't move, then with deep sigh he admitted that he had fallen in love with her. But he knew the difference between being in love and loving someone. He hoped one would lead to the other. With that thought, he returned to the Battalion Area and his bunk.

* * *

There were now forty trucks in Leo the Tiger's convoy, including tankers from two different oil companies. But when General Lewis was told they were heading for Fort Bliss, he immediately issued orders to the MP Detachment to stop the convoy from entering Federal property. This was quickly relayed to Louie the Tiger by friends inside Bliss, and he immediately stopped the convoy, found a phone booth and called the Boss, who told him not to worry and to proceed as planned.

The Boss called several friends in Washington, who in turn called their friends in the War Department and within twenty minutes of Louie's call to the Boss, General Cannon received a phone call from General Wackham, Chief of Personnel, who made it quite clear that his new command can quickly become his old command, or still worse, his last command if he persisted in his unfriendly attitude toward the FEED OUR MEN convoy. There were no "ifs or buts" about it.

The phone call had such an effect on the General that he beat his mahogany desk with his swagger stick until it was reduced to splinters and the desk was badly scarred. Then he went to the Officers Club, drank three straight Martinees, and then went out to meet Louie the Tiger, whose jeep was parked directly in front the Headquarters Building.

Louie took one look at Lewis, and turning to the men behind, he said in Italian, "The big shit don't look happy."

The men laughed.

Louie got out of the Jeep and faced Lewis, who was directly in front of him. "Tell me where the Two-Forty-Fifth Infantry Battalion is."

"Up in the mountains by now," the General answered.

Louie looked around him. "There's lots of fuckin' mountain around here," he said.

"Pick one," Lewis said.

"Listen, and listen good General, I got you by your balls. You don't play ball with me, you're fuckin' out of here, *capisce*?"

Lewis blanched. No one ever spoke to him that way.

"I need two guides, just in case one of them develops a case of the losts." Louis said.

"You don't waste much time or words," Lewis answered.

"You got that right, General; so get me those guides like two hours ago," Louis said

Lewis's face was purple, but he nodded, did a smart "about face" and retreated into headquarters, while Louie the Tiger bit the end off of a cigar before lighting up and said, "We ought to run the fuckin' army. We'd do a better job of it than a shithead like that."

* * *

Getting to the Cunt was hairy no matter how you approached it. From its front, there was a narrow switch-back road that ended two hundred feet below the entrance to the pass. From its rear, a mountain goat would have difficulty getting to it.

Initially, Captain Peter Grinder commander of the two 82nd Airborne Troops was primed to make a surprise drop, seize the high ground on both sides of the pass, effectively neutralizing any defense the 245th could mount.

But the gods of war are fickle, even when they're playing games. Grinder had his men in two C-54s, and ready to drop when he received word that a freak snow-storm was rapidly approaching the drop-zone.

And at the same time, Louie, who managed to commandeer an army radio, heard a similar message emanating from the Meteorological Station at Bliss and also from the El Paso Airport. Grinder and Louie were faced with roughly the same problem: continue or turn back. Grinder took the position that exercise wouldn't last long once his men had control of the high ground; and Louie held, "Snow or no snow, the men have to be fed."

While these two men were deciding what course of action to take, the 245th Infantry Battalion suddenly found itself engulfed by swirling snow, freezing temperatures and they were only two thousand feet up; and none of the men wore anything more than their summer uniforms and light field jackets.

Colonel Miller radioed his situation to Base Headquarters and requested permission to abort the mission.

General Cannon denied the request on the grounds that a unit should be able to function no matter what the weather conditions were.

Grinder, on hearing Cannon's radioed response was even more determined to carry out his end of the mission.

Pilots of the two C54s were anxious to unload their cargo, and to return to the base to watch the storm from a place where the sun was warm and the drinks plentiful. "Okay, Captain, we're approaching the DZ."

"Roger, that," Grinder answered, and ordered the Jump Master to ready the men.

Moments later the doors on both aircraft were opened. The men stood up and attached themselves to the static line. The green light flashed and one after another they leaped out of the aircraft. Above them the sky was a brilliant blue, but beneath them it was an ugly mix of grays verging on black.

They too were not accoutered for a winter exercise. The wind grabbed them and pushed them west of the DZ.

The 245th's lead vehicle, the Jeep with Miller, Davidson and Connelly in it, reached the end of the narrow roadway and couldn't go any further because of drifting snow.

"From this point, everything has to be man handled," Miller announced, and immediately gave the order to stake out the defense perimeter, according to the Ops directives prepared by Sergeant Katz and Major Connelly. And so the men began to unload the trucks, and drag the necessary equipment into place.

The first tent to go up was Headquarters, a very large edifice that offered protection against the snow and the wind, but not the cold. All the units' field stoves were put in that tent and lit to provide heat and to enable the cooks and bakers to prepare hot food for the men. Slowly more tents were put up, and the men began to take up their designated positions.

By early afternoon, a foot of snow had fallen and the forecast was the same for the next thirty-six hours, with temperatures well below freezing during the day, and an expectation of ten to fifteen degrees below zero at night.

Miller called all his officers together and said, "We're in a critical situation."

The silence that followed was equivalent to an answer of, "No shit, Colonel. Tell us something we didn't know."

Miller was about to speak again when one of the men on the outside of the tent yelled, "More trucks comin' up the road."

The customary look of confusion took over Miller's face, and as if it was a virus, it quickly spread to the faces of his subordinates. Miller was reluctant to leave the warmth of the tent to find out who the new arrivals were. They certainly wouldn't be the attacking forces, who were not expected to attack until the storm blew itself out. Even if they did attack during the storm, they wouldn't get very far before the drifting snow would stop them.

Suddenly the tent flap was pushed back and Leo and his four bodyguards entered. And he whooped, "Hey Miller what the hell are you doin' here?"

Leo recognized Miller from the track. They both went to Belmont Race Track in Nassau County on Long Island to watch the races or the Trotters.

"What the hell are you doing here?" Miller asked.

"Got food and vino for your men," Leo said. "Forty fuckin' truck loads. Enough for couple of real good feeds. The fuckin' army shouldn't keep you on short rations. No. No. This is America. The guys in uniform should have the best of what we have."

Miller nodded dumbly.

"Hey guys, my name is Leo," he told the other men; then spotting Celenza, he ran over to him and kissed him on both cheeks. "Your mama and papa were so worried that you weren't gettin' enough to eat."

Celenza stood absolutely motionless.

"Trappaso is the man I gotta find," Leo said. "Angie told her papa about the short rations, and he told me. And I decided to do somethin' about it, so, here I am. My guys are already setting up. In a couple hours everyone will have steak-pizziola, and spaghetti with meat sauce, coffee and vino."

"But—"

"You don't have to thank me" Leo said. "I do the right thing when the right thing has to be done. Ask anyone in Bath Beach, Brooklyn who gives away more turkeys on Thanksgiving or hams on Christmas and Easter and they'll tell you Leo does."

Just as he finished speaking, Captain Grinder and two of his men practically fell into the tent. Grinder was in tears, "It's all lost; my men are scattered."

Despite his emotional state, Grinder was able to explain who he was, and what his mission was.

"Well, we can't hold that against you," Leo said, adding, "but you're lucky."

"Lucky?"

"Sure lucky, you and your men are prisoners of the 245th, and not a shot has been fired. And you get to eat some the best Italian food you'd find only in Italy and drink the best Italian wine. So, instead of freezing your ass off, you and your men will be warm." He looked at Miller and asked, "Isn't that right?"

Miller looked at Davidson, who nodded.

"Yea, that's right," Miller said.

"Okay, we're cookin'," Leo said and he and his bodyguard walked out of there leaving Miller and his officers wondering what they'd just experienced: the beneficence of a truly good man, a miracle, or the work of the devil for those who believed in him. Regardless of which one it was, they were in no position to refuse the largess offered to them.

More stragglers from the 82nd came into the tent, willingly surrendered, and enjoyed the food and wine. Luckily, the two platoons didn't lose a man and Grinder was their hero for having found the 245th Infantry Battalion and the surfeit of food and drink it offered them.

* * *

Silvia and Angie met several times to discuss their peculiar situation while their husbands were on maneuvers. The meetings were emotionally difficult for them. They had fallen in love with each other in a way that neither one of them expected. And both realized that it was "beyond the boundary" of what was considered normal. Both loved their husbands but not in the same way that they loved each other. Both enjoyed having sex with their husbands, but not the same way that they enjoyed it with each other. Both swore to avoid any physical contact with each other that would lead them to the bedroom. But just seeing one another across a lunch table was enough for each of them to forswear what they had sworn not to do.

Each of them realized they would have to hide their lesbian proclivities behind a mask of ordinariness, that any change might arouse the suspicions of their husbands. And in addition to the terrible beating that they expected would follow, they would lose everything including their children.

It was the kind of situation they would have wished not to be in, but it was the situation they were in, and for the first time in their lives, they had an emotional reality they had to face and come terms with, and they did: first by realizing they had a problem and then by realizing that people have all sorts of problems that they have to cope with, have to mask in some way in order to live a "normal life."

Having reached this decision, they finished their lunch and then drove to a nearby motel, where they spent a delightful two hours together before going home.

* * *

The army is very skittish about losing men, misplacing them. They have hundreds of men—if not a couple of thousand—whose job it is to know where every man is—what unit he is in—every moment of every day, in our terms of time, 24/7.

So when four hundred men who were due in New York at a specific date for deployment to the 4th Division in Germany failed to show up, those whose task it was to keep track of troop movements were perplexed in the extreme. That they might have been hijacked by the enemy—recall that we were at war with North Korea—was given some consideration, but rejected because it would have been impossible to move them out of the country without someone noticing.

So that put them in country, but where?

They mystery remained a mystery, confounding those in command of Army Personnel, causing them to hold special meetings, and detail hundreds of men to scan thousands of sheets of paper for the slightest clue. And then quite by accident, a lowly corporal noticed that infantry unit, namely the 245th Infantry Battalion, was assigned to Fort Bliss, an artillery base. And this lowly corporal, whose name was Arduno Pertraogia, had read in the Washington Herald two news worthy events: the first having to do with breach of security information that would soon be investigated by HUAC, and the second, closer to the search for the missing four hundred men, because it involved a movement called FEED THE MEN, whose avowed purpose was to bring food to the 245th Infantry Battalion because the unit had been on half rations as a result of a sudden influx of men that the commissary at Bliss would not acknowledge without the proper paper work.

Arduno brought this information to his Sergeant, who passed it to a Lieutenant, and from him it went up the chain of command to General Quick Biscuit, who unfortunately, despite his given name, was not at all that quick and held his position because his uncle was a Senator from Delaware, where Senators and Congressmen are also employed by the country's major chemical manufacturers. But his aide, Colonel George Basset, saw the connection and patiently explained it to the General.

The General said, "I want to meet the corporal before we go any further."

And so Arduno was summoned from the nether regions where he and others like him moiled to the General's office, which was located on the top floor of the building.

The General looked at Arduno and Arduno looked at the General. Neither was able to believe what they were looking at. Arduno had never seen the General before, and now that he was looking at him, he was surprised that the General was a fat middle aged man, who wore metal frame glasses and was bald. He looked as if he were someone's uncle, a bachelor who still lived with his mother.

At the same time Arduno was gathering these impressions, the General looked over the rim of his glasses at a short, dark skinned young man and guessed he was Italian or Spanish, and no doubt a draftee.

"Corporal Pertragoia, from this moment on, you is Sergeant Pertraogia," the General announced with a big smile. The orders will be cut this afternoon and will be retroactive to the first of the month."

"Thank you, Sir," Arduno responded.

"Now tell me how you figured out where those four hundred men were?"

Arduno walked the General through the various steps in his reasoning, but had to repeat himself many times because the General had difficulty following his explanation.

"You're a college graduate, aren't you?"

"Yes, Sir."

The General nodded. He was too, but just barely. He was at the bottom of his class. That fact made him choose the army for his career where a lot of bottoms become the tops. And after a long pause, he said, "Well, now that we know where the men are we have to get them."

"Yes, Sir," Arduno said.

The General turned to his aide, Colonel John Dice, and said, "I want those men on their way by oh seven hundred tomorrow."

"Yes, Sir," Dice answered.

"And Sergeant, I want you close by," the General said. "I need a man like you to help me think."

* * *

When General Loose Cannon was told that the 245th had four hundred men who were initially assigned to the 4th Division in Germany, he was so taken-aback that he was speechless until he remembered that the 245th was up at the Cunt, and was snowed in. At that point he began to scream and beat his desk with a new swagger stick that soon reduced to splinters.

"I want every snowplow we have up there," he shouted. "The road has to be opened."

"We don't have any snowplows, Sir," his aide said.

"No snow plows?" The General asked looking like a child who had just been denied his favorite cookie.

"It seldom snows here and when it does, it's gone within a matter of hours."

"El Paso—" the General began hopefully.

"No, Sir."

"Are you telling me they're going to be up in the Cunt until spring time?"

"No, Sir."

"Leo has arranged for snow plows to be flown in from New York. They're in the air even as we speak."

"Just how the fuck did he do that?"

His aide shrugged. "Whoever or whatever he's connected to are better organized than we are, and that's a fact."

"Goddam, I need a drink," the General said.

"I could use one or two myself," his Aide answered.

"Good," Loose Cannon said, and pulled a bottle of scotch out of the bottom drawer of his desk.

CHAPTER XI

It snowed for three days and three nights, so that by the time that Leo's snow plows arrived at the El Paso International Airport—the aircraft carrying them was not permitted to land at Biggs Air Force Base—there was nine feet of snow on the road above the thousand foot level and the men of the 245th moved from place on Cunt in tunnels of their own making.

During this time, Leo got to know many of the men in Celenza's Company, play cards with Miller, and let him win a few hands before he blitzed him for a G, mostly in IOU's. He hated being inactive and found little to relive his boredom. But he spent a lot of time listing to the chatter on the military radio he had obtained. Some of what he heard was coded, but much of it wasn't; and because he knew that the first troops out of the snow-bound 245th would be the four hundred men that the 4th Division in Germany was eagerly waiting for. This piece of information was like "manna from heaven" for the Israelites in the desert. But there were two essential differences: the 245th wasn't in the desert and they weren't by any stretch of his or anyone else's imagination Israelites. To Leo that didn't matter; manna was manna, especially if it came in the form of money; and that was exactly the way he interpreted the information he heard on the radio because it sparked an incredible idea that would enhance his standing with the "Boss," and extend his own reach from the Bath Beach and Mill Basin areas in Brooklyn to other areas in the borough that would be more lucrative, especially to his numbers game and protection scam. To achieve that, he needed something big and it was dropped in to his lap, to be more exact his ears. Four hundred men had four hundred rifles that they would not take with them when they left. Those rifles could easily go missing just like the men went missing. The army was always losing things and writing off the losses as part of doing business, being the army. In mint condition they were worth a "tidy bundle." But to do it, he needed someone "on the inside" whose presence would make it look legitimate when each of the rifles would be picked up by one of his men. Perhaps even give a phony receipt for the rifle.

Realizing the odds for such an opportunity to come again were enormous, his choice of the "inside man" had to be someone with smarts, who was willing to take the risk for a cut of the take, probable, as he figured it, ten percent.

To implement his plan, he called Frank and Giorgio, his two trusted lieutenants for a confab, handing each a Mancanoodo cigar before he began to lay out his plan.

The men listened attentively, blowing a lot smoke as they did.

When he was finished with his explanation, Leo asked, "So what's your take on it?"

Both men nodded and Frank said, "Brilliant."

And Giorgio said, "Brilliant, boss; but it ain't goin' to work."

Leo took the cigar out of his mouth, squinted at Giorgio and asked, "Why the fuck not?"

"The men don't have the rifles," Giorgio answered.

Leo looked Frank.

"Yeah, boss; they no have them," Frank answered.

Leo left the camp chair he sat on and began to pace. "Tell me how soldiers can't have his gun, his rifle."

"They weren't issued any. Like the food there was a shortage. Only enough for the men—"

Leo stopped and smacked his head. Celenza had explained all about the TOE. "That's the trouble with the fuckin' army, they got all these tables, all these rules...And there, I thought I had it covered.

The both men nodded their heads in commiseration.

"Here, I am wit time on my hands and I can't do anything wid it," Leo complained. "It's just getting harder and harder to make a buck."

* * *

The weather cleared; the sun came out and turned the snow into water; and the water created mud and waterfalls. The waterfalls washed out the switch-back road and the made life at the Cunt a dirty business. But eventually the engineers from Bliss were able to sufficiently rebuild the switch-back roadway to allow the convoy of four hundred men to leave. They weren't sorry to leave and the men in the 245th weren't sorry to see them go.

During the second day of the unit's forced incarceration, Gibbs, made up with Polly, and decided to give MacKenna what he wanted. They found him at his portable desk in a makeshift area in one corner of the CommandTent. He took the book without comment. But Gibbs said, "We're now a threesome."

MacKenna didn't answer; and whatever Gibbs and Polly expected to happen, didn't happen either, leaving the two of them speechless.

* * *

Two days later, the mud bespattered 245th came off the mountain and rolled into their camp site on Logan Heights. Because of the condition of the men and the equipment, General Loose Cannon gave them three days of down time to rest, get cleaned up and clean the equipment. Getting cleaned up was the most difficult part: the showers, special runs to the laundry and sleeping occupied most of the first day.

By the second day, MacKenna appropriated Davidson's office and wore the uniform of his rightful rank, that of a full Colonel. Polly and Gibbs was summoned asp to the office, and when they entered the found themselves looking at the back of someone who they thought was Major Davidson. But when he turned and they saw who it was, both men staggered. Had either of them known Shakespeare's *Hamlet*, one of them might whispered, "Oh my prophetic soul," but neither of them did, and looked at the man behind the desk as if they were hypnotized by him and in a way they were.

"CID," MacKenna said with a smile. But the smile quickly vanished, and he said, "I have enough evidence to for a Courts Martial to give each of you twenty years at hard labor. But because I don't think that would achieve anything positive this is what's going to happen: Gibbs, effective immediately you are being transferred to a unit in the Aleutian Islands; your rank will remain the same but you'll be working under a Master - Master Sergeant and if you step out of line -- well, I'll leave that to the people in that command. As for you, Polly, you will be sent to cryptography school and then rejoin the unit in Korea. As for your present bankroll, all of it will be donated to the Army Fund, leaving you with nothing but your army pay. There isn't any way for either of you to appeal these decisions. They were made on the command level to make maximum use of each of you for the benefit of the army. Dismissed."

MacKenna waited until the two miscreants left before he picked up the phone and dialed Flo's number. Life was looking real good, better when she answered and said, "I love you."

"Me too," Mackenna told her. "Me too."

* * *

And so, to speak in Shakespearean terms, "all's well that ends well." The army as portrayed never existed, and yet there will be veterans who when reading about the 245th Infantry Battalion will no doubt smile as they recognize some small part of their own experience or identify someone similar to a character in the fictional-reality of the story.